Mastering the Academic Writing Mindset

Tsz Nam Chan · Dingming Wu

Mastering the Academic Writing Mindset

A Guide to Crafting Computer Science Papers

 Springer

Tsz Nam Chan
College of Computer Science and Software
Engineering
Shenzhen University
Shenzhen, China

Dingming Wu
College of Computer Science and Software
Engineering
Shenzhen University
Shenzhen, China

ISBN 978-981-95-4849-1   ISBN 978-981-95-4850-7 (eBook)
https://doi.org/10.1007/978-981-95-4850-7

This work was supported by Shenzhen University and National Natural Science Foundation of China.

This Springer imprint is published by the registered company Springer Nature Singapore Pte Ltd.
The registered company address is: 152 Beach Road, #21-01/04 Gateway East, Singapore 189721, Singapore

If disposing of this product, please recycle the paper.

Preface

Many postgraduate students (especially junior postgraduate students) are struggling to write research papers. Although many postgraduate students have solid background and are passionate for conducting research, some of them can have no progress for submitting papers in several months (or even years), causing anxiety. Worse still, the more anxiety they experience, the less they submit, which further creates a vicious cycle. Ultimately, they may leave the academia forever, leading to a loss of talents. However, the main reason for those students to have no progress is that they may initially have wrong mindsets for academic writing. Therefore, this book aims to provide our first-hand experience for conducting research in the computer science field. As an evidence, the first author, Tsz Nam Chan, also seriously suffered from procrastination during his Ph.D. study (from 1st July 2014 to 15th March 2019) and graduated with only three first-author research papers. By mastering the correct mindset, he published nearly 20 research papers as a first author in top-tier venues, including Proceedings of ACM Conference on Management of Data (SIGMOD), Proceedings of the VLDB Endowment (VLDB), IEEE International Conference on Data Engineering (ICDE), and IEEE Transactions on Knowledge and Data Engineering (TKDE), within a short period of time (the number of first-author papers changes from 3 to 20 starting from 15th March 2019 to 1st May 2025), and received the title of National Science Fund for Excellent Young Scholars (Overseas), which is a prestigious title in China, with the age of 32.

In this book, we will first discuss some common mistakes regarding research attitudes and research actions that are made by new postgraduate students and the corresponding correct mindsets. Then, we will discuss some common mistakes related to reading and writing attitudes and paper presentation and point out the correct mindset for each of these mistakes. Lastly, we will further discuss how to enhance the chance for making a paper accepted in a top-tier venue.

Shenzhen, China
May 2025
Tsz Nam Chan
Dingming Wu

Acknowledgements This book is supported in part by the National Natural Science Foundation of China under Grants 23IAA00610, 62572326, 62202401, and 62372308, the GuangDong Basic and Applied Basic Research Foundation under Grant 2023A1515011619, Scientific Foundation for Youth Scholars of Shenzhen University, and Shenzhen University Excellent Graduate-Level Teaching Materials Project. We would also like to say thank you to the designer Xiao Ma for re-drawing those beautiful figures in this book.

Contents

Chapter 1
Background

In recent years, gradually more students with bachelor degrees of computer science and its related field would like to undertake postgraduate studies (e.g., MPhil and Ph.D.), especially for countries in Far East (e.g., China, South Korea, Singapore, and Japan). According to the news in Global Times, the number of postgraduate students (on campus) in China steadily increases in the twenty-first century, which has already reached 3.65 million in 2022 (see Fig. 1.1).

However, many students, including the ones who achieve high GPAs in undergraduate studies, are struggled with postgraduate studies. They may even leave the academia forever, leading to the loss of talents. The main reason for this kind of failure is that those students do not understand the differences between undergraduate studies and postgraduate studies. Therefore, they still adopt the previous (successful) mindsets in the undergraduate studies for the postgraduate studies, which can ultimately be failure.

During the undergraduate study, each student needs to take a lot of fundamental courses (e.g., C++ programming, data structures, design and analysis of algorithms, linear algebra, multivariate calculus, and probability and statistics). In order to be successful (i.e., get a high grade) in these courses, all they need to do is to (1) attend classes, (2) listen carefully in each class, (3) do a lot of exercises after each class, (4) submit assignments on time, (5) know the scope of each examination, and (6) prepare well for each examination. Note that these six steps are mainly used to consolidate their foundations, which are (of course) important. However, they are nothing related to the creativity issue. As an example, all problems (or exercises) are either provided by lecturers or obtained from textbooks, meaning that the students do not need to think of a new problem. As another example, solutions to these problems must be within the scopes of examinations (or textbooks). Therefore, the students can easily figure out the correct (and probably unique) solution to each problem.

However, most of the above steps are no longer useful during the postgraduate study since we do not use the traditional examination to measure the research outcome. Instead, each student needs to find his/her own research problem, motivate the research problem (by telling a good story of it), figure out the solution for

Fig. 1.1 The number of Chinese students on campus in 2022 has already reached 3.65 million (obtained from the news in Global Times)

this problem, and write a research paper related to this problem in order to make it accepted in the prestigious conferences/journals. As such, there are many critical changes in this stage. First, those research problems may not be given (or clearly provided). The MPhil/Ph.D. supervisors sometimes may just have a rough direction (e.g., non-parametric density estimation models are very slow, which are worth for investigation.). Worse still, some supervisors (especially for those tenured professors who need to handle a lot of administrative issues from the universities, have various meetings every day, and become lazy) may not be on the front line of research and cannot provide clear directions. Therefore, the student needs to actively find the new research problem by himself/herself. Second, after the student finds the research problem, he/she cannot figure out one arbitrary solution (just like submitting an assignment to the lecturer). Instead, they need to develop a solution that can clearly advance the state of the art, which means this solution must be demonstrated to be better than the existing solutions in some aspects. Furthermore, these new solutions are unlikely to be bounded by the scopes from textbooks (or examinations). Third, the student needs to write an academic paper to present the problem and its motivation, the related studies, the new solution, the experimental results, and the conclusion in a logical way so that reviewers in top-tier conferences/journals can accept it. Note that many universities do not offer this kind of training in the undergraduate studies. Fourth, many students mainly rely on the lecturer for each course. For example, they may wait for the lecturer to provide the assignments for them to finish in order to get the high grade. However, the MPhil/Ph.D. supervisors may not be reliable (as mentioned above, they may have a lot of administrative issues). As such, the student needs to learn how to work independently.[1]

With the above changes, many students may not be comfortable. Many of them do not know what to do next in the first year. Even worse, some students may get

---

[1] This is also an important skill for a university to determine whether it needs to hire that student to be a faculty member.

lost in the whole period of the postgraduate studies (e.g., zero publication in four years). In the worst situation, a few of them may even suffer from depression due to the zero progress of research. We believe that some of these students are really the talents and work extremely hard toward their research. However, they have nearly no progress because of their (initially) incorrect mindsets, which should be addressed in the very early stage. Therefore, in Chaps. 2 and 3, we first discuss common mistakes related to research attitudes and research actions, respectively, and point out the corresponding correct mindsets. Then, in Chaps. 4 and 5, we further discuss common mistakes regarding the reading and writing attitudes and presenting research papers, respectively, and the corresponding correct mindsets. Lastly, we discuss how to enhance the chance for making a paper accepted in a top-tier venue in Chap. 6.

Chapter 2
Common Mistakes and Correct Mindsets for Research Attitudes

In this chapter, we discuss some common mistakes for research attitudes that have been made by new postgraduate students (including us in the early stage of career), which have been categorized into the following nine types. The correct mindset will be discussed for each type of the mistakes.

2.1 Only "Fulfill" the Tasks from Supervisors

Many students may only "fulfill" the tasks from supervisors without having any motivation for conducting research. Here is the mindset of those students.

"If the supervisor tells me to do it, I will do it. I will only syntactically "fulfill" his/her instruction. If the supervisor does not tell me to do it, I will never think about it." (see Fig. 2.1)

This kind of mindset is similar to submitting an assignment to a course lecturer or fulfilling the tasks from a boss in a company.

However, this mindset must not be adopted for conducting research. Instead, students should regard research as something they need to be fully dedicated to. They need to love it as they love their boyfriends/girlfriends/sons/daughters. Using Fig. 2.2 as an example, even though the supervisor has provided one direction (XXX in this example), the student should think in a deeper way for how to further improve this paper, e.g., revise this paper thoroughly and continuously improve this work (add YYY in this example). Here, we need to emphasize that every student must have the following mindset.

Students should be mainly responsible for their research (not their supervisors). Supervisors only need to assist their research. In other words, students must be able to in charge of everything related to their own research, including (1) finding a research problem, (2) motivating this problem, (3) developing state-of-the-art solutions, (4) conducting experiments, (5) writing a research paper

© The Author(s) 2026
T. N. Chan and D. Wu, *Mastering the Academic Writing Mindset*,
https://doi.org/10.1007/978-981-95-4850-7_2

Fig. 2.1 Unproductive students simply "fulfill" the tasks by their supervisors

independently, and (6) dealing with comments from reviewers in top-tier venues independently. Figure 2.3 **shows how to be a qualified Ph.D. student.**

2.2 Wait Around for Next Tasks

Many students may just regard conducting research as a job in a company, which means that they will only finish those tasks given by their supervisors. However, after they have finished them, they will never ask any additional questions. As an example, suppose that the supervisor has given the student the task for conducting an experiment, the student may just finish it in a few days and do nothing in the next few days (like the case in Fig. 2.4). As another example, suppose that the supervisor has asked the student to read one research paper. The student simply reads it and does not explore other related papers in the literature.

Fig. 2.2 Productive students love their research work

Fig. 2.3 A qualified Ph.D. student must reach this level

Here, we need to emphasize that this mindset (or attitude) is wrong. Conducting research is not the same as a 9am–5pm job in a company. Research papers should be regarded as your asset. The main reasons are that (1) research papers are forever, which can be downloaded by everyone in the world, (2) your name is on those research papers, which means that everyone can know you (this is a glory for you), and (3) each top-tier paper can significantly help you find a tenure-track position/the best of the best research lab position (top-tier papers = money). Therefore, you

Fig. 2.4 A student just waits for his/her supervisor to provide the next task

should not simply wait for your supervisors to provide you the next task (especially when the meeting time is normally short, which does not allow a busy supervisor who has supervised many postgraduate students to provide extremely comprehensive comments). Instead, you need to lead your own research (keep pushing it) and ask for your supervisor help when you get stuck (see Fig. 2.5).

2.3 Pretend to Understand

Many postgraduate students are normally the best of the best students during their undergraduate studies (e.g., receive the first-class honors). Therefore, some of these students may not be able to accept the fact that they cannot understand somethings in research papers (see Fig. 2.6). They may pretend to understand them during the meeting with others (most probably their supervisors). The main reason is that admitting the failure of understanding somethings may reveal their weakness, which can harm their prides. For those students, we would like to emphasize that this mindset is wrong. First, research papers in top-tier venues are written by researchers with

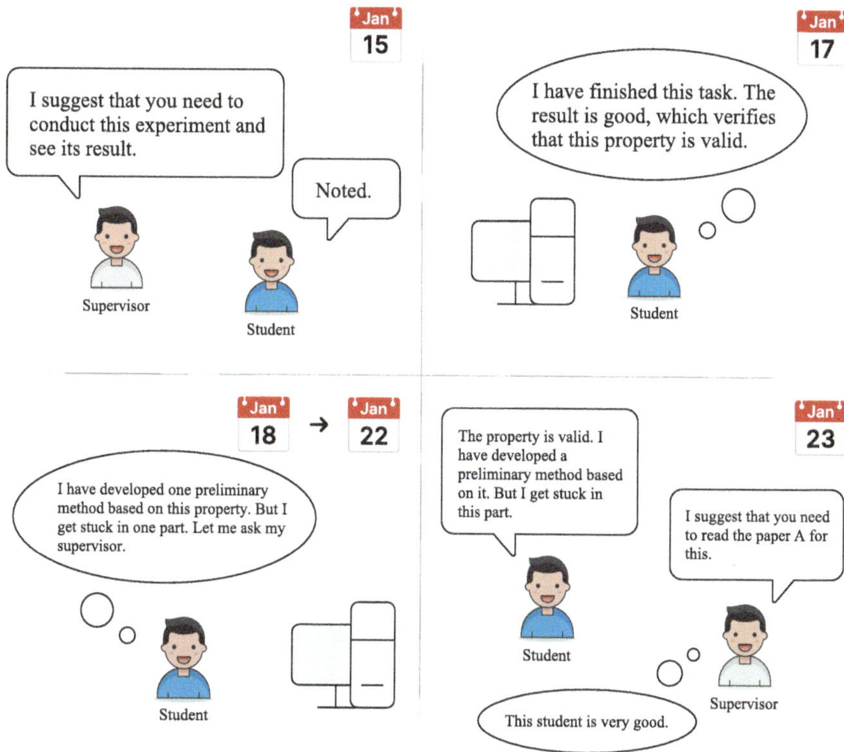

Fig. 2.5 A student should lead his/her own research, without waiting for his/her supervisor

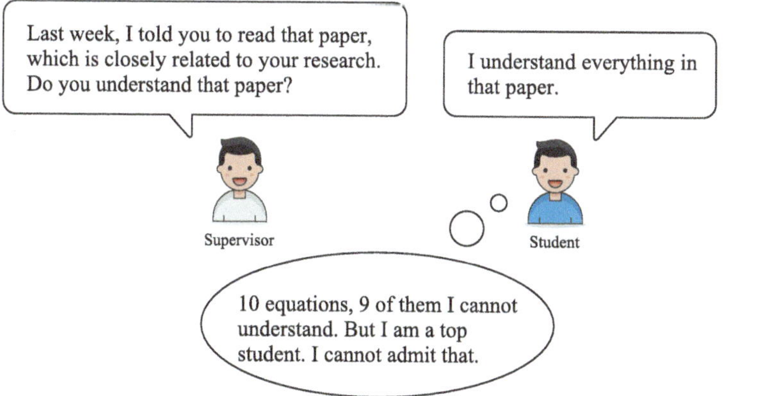

Ending: No progress in the following month. The supervisor discovers that this student does not understand everything and blames him/her seriously.

Fig. 2.6 A student that pretends to understand can slow down the progress of his/her research

Ending: The supervisor provides suggestions. The student understands the concepts of that paper and continues further research.

Fig. 2.7 A student should admit that he/she does not understand in order to understand

rich experience. Therefore, it is possible that these papers are hard to be digested by a newbie, who does not equip with enough background knowledge. Second, if students pretend to understand somethings, the supervisors cannot determine the real progress of those students, which can significantly slow down the research progress.

In contrast, if those students can admit that they cannot understand the papers (see Fig. 2.7), their supervisors can easily identify where the students get stuck in order to provide corresponding suggestions for them. With these suggestions, the students can pass through the difficulties (i.e., earn more experience) and continue their research smoothly.

2.4 Never Believe in Their Work

Many unproductive students would frequently change from one topic to another topic when they have encountered some issues that are difficult to solve. They normally provide many "reasons" (we think these are just excuses) for changing topics (see Fig. 2.8).

Reason 1 (The topic is boring.): Some students may be very enthusiastic in the first few weeks after they have found their new research topics that they are eager to work on. However, after these students suffer from several difficulties in three to six months (Here are some possible examples. (1) It is hard to implement existing solutions. (2) There are plenty of related research papers that they cannot understand. (3) It is hard to develop a good solution. (4) It is hard to write a draft about this topic that can make their supervisors feel happy.), they will start feeling bored about this topic. At the same time, they can even grumble about why they choose this "stupid" topic before and start shifting from one research topic to another research topic when they see some new research papers that look fancy to them. For these students, we need to emphasize that **no research topic is easy.** They must encounter some difficulties

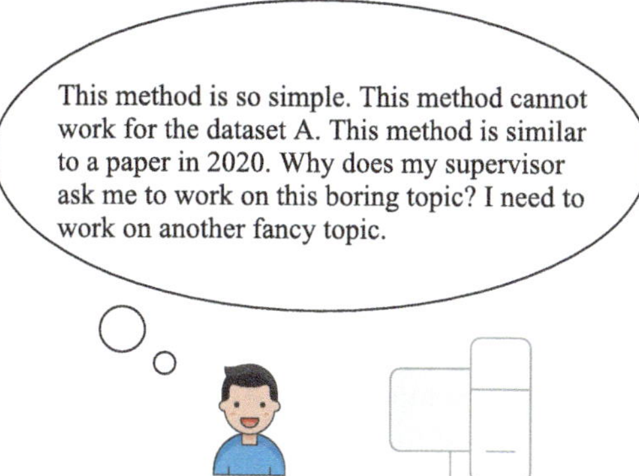

Ending: Moves to the next topic and still fails to produce anything. Ultimately kicked out by his/her supervisor.

Fig. 2.8 Unproductive students do not believe in their work

when they conduct research for any topic. Even though they change to another fancy topic (i.e., avoid the painful experience of the previous topic), it is likely for them to feel bored after they encounter difficulties for the new topic. Therefore, the students should stick to this topic (especially when this topic is found by them) until they have finished working on it (by submitting a paper to a prestigious venue (see Fig. 2.9)). Otherwise, it can waste the precious time (e.g., three to six months) that they (and their supervisors) contribute before.

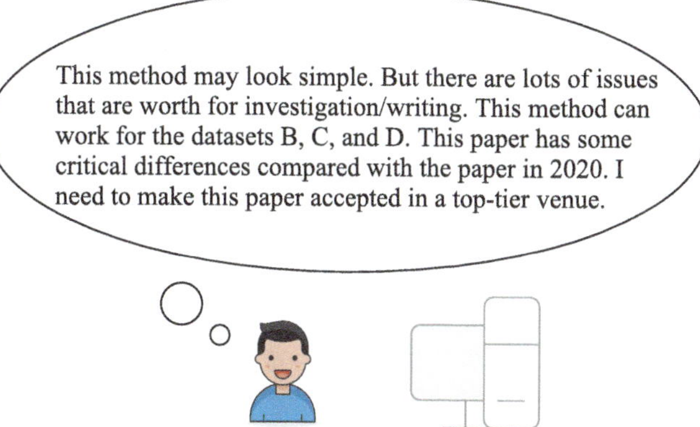

Ending: Makes this paper accepted in a top-tier venue. Graduates with five top-tier papers.

Fig. 2.9 Productive students believe in their work

Reason 2 (The method is so simple.): Some students have developed a new method for their research topics and think that this method is so simple that is not worth for publication. Although their supervisors ask them to write down this method in the draft, they will not be very motivated for this task. Due to the weak motivation, they will not ask additional questions that can possibly remedy this (Here are some possible examples. (1) Can this simple method have some theoretical guarantees? (2) Can they support more useful problem settings? (Note that the method may need to be significantly revised for a new problem setting.)). For these students, we need to point out that publishing a research paper (1) does not mean we need to develop some solutions that look very complicated and are full of mathematics/pseudocodes and (2) does not mean we need to make somethings that can significantly change the world (e.g., formulate the equation $E = mc^2$). Furthermore, **a simple method does not mean that it is not worth for publication.** When you take a look for those publications in top-tier venues recently, many papers reuse ideas from those papers published in several decades ago. But why are these papers accepted? It is mainly because these papers (1) advance the state of the art in new problem settings, (2) have a good story (i.e., good abstract and introduction), (3) are well-written, and (4) are very comprehensive. In order to make these papers accepted in prestigious venues, all we need to do is to be motivated and keep asking questions to push this paper forward every day (see Fig. 2.9).

Reason 3 (The method cannot work for some datasets.): After students have run some experiments for testing their methods, they may find that the experimental results may not be good for some datasets. At that time, the students can feel very frustrated and think that their methods are not good in practice. Some students can immediately lose the motivation and keep saying somethings negative. Here are some possible examples. (1) This method does not work. (2) I need to develop a new method from scratch, which takes a lot of time, and I am not confident about this. Can I shift to the next topic? (3) I may not be suitable for conducting research. Let me find a job in industry. For these students, we need to emphasize that **this is not the end of the world if the experimental results are not good.** There are many approaches that can remedy this. We need to know that each method can have good performance in some datasets, while it can have weak performance in other datasets. Therefore, it is quite hard to develop a method that can achieve good performance for all datasets. Instead of designing another method from scratch, students should ask this question first. Which dataset properties are suitable for their methods? By figuring out the answers, they can select the correct datasets for conducting experiments (see Fig. 2.9). In addition, it is possible for them to develop a new theory/discover a new research direction behind that. As an example, suppose that the research question is to develop efficient algorithms for handling one computational problem. If the new method can only be efficient for handling sparse datasets compared with existing methods, the student should ask whether they can make the original (dense) dataset sparse without affecting the accuracy of solving the computational problem. He/she should not give up this method based on this kind of "weakness" (i.e., cannot efficiently handle dense datasets).

Reason 4 (The method is similar to a paper that was published several years ago.): Many students may discover that some methods in published papers are quite similar to their methods when they conduct literature review. After they find those papers that are similar to their ongoing papers, they will be very upset and think that this is the end of the world. They will also become not motivated for asking further questions and immediately give up this topic. For these students, we would like to ask them this question. Are these two papers really similar to each other? Previously, we supervise one student. In one meeting with this student, we discuss a new idea for solving a research problem. Then, the student keeps saying that this idea is the same as one previous research paper. But when we ask him which part is the same? He only says that the idea has one tiny part (which is hard for anyone to think of) that is the similar to that paper. Come on. Most of the ideas should be somehow similar to previous one. Therefore, how can this tiny part be interpreted as "the same idea"? As an example, suppose that we aim to utilize the compression approach for solving one computational problem. Then, can we say that this approach is the same as every compression solution? Obviously no. It is because we need to utilize the properties of the computational problem, which is the new thing, in order to develop our compression approach. **Therefore, instead of being frustrated of the similarity between two papers and using this to attack the proposed idea, the students should try to find the differences (show the novelty) in order to attack the published paper (see Fig.** 2.9).

2.5 Think That the Research Community is Ideal

Some students may think that conducting research is similar to some scientists in TV shows/movies, which depict that they are extremely hard to get one paper accepted. Each acceptance must be a breakthrough (e.g., from 5G to 6G, from weak AI to strong AI, or other Turing-award worthy/Nobel-prize worthy work). Therefore, they think that they need to spend three to four years to get only one paper accepted in a top-tier conference/journal. To be honest, these students may be idealistic (see Fig. 2.10). Normally, these students can feel very frustrated during the postgraduate studies especially when they see that (1) some colleagues can manage to publish three to four papers in top-tier venues per year and (2) those research papers in the literature are not really good (or even cannot reach the level that the authors claim before). Using the first author of this book as an example, he tried to reproduce the experimental results from one paper about manifold learning that was published in a very top-tier venue. At that time, he believed that every paper in a top-tier venue must be a kind of glory, which must be better than existing methods in all sides. However, after he conducted the experiments, he did not receive the good results as claimed by that paper. He was very frustrated and debugged the code for a long time but still could not obtain the results. Nine months later, he was fortunate to attend a top-tier conference with the first author of that paper. The author mentioned that there are some hidden assumptions in that paper and apologized to him. Therefore, we need to

Fig. 2.10 Students that are idealistic may be very disappointed about the research community

point out that a research paper (by extension to a research community) is not ideal at all. Instead of having serious complaints about the research community, we believe that those students need to reduce the expectation in their minds (i.e., accept the fact that it is not ideal).

2.6 Think That Only Extraordinary Work Can Be Accepted in Top-Tier Venues

Many students would think that the level of a top-tier venue in computer science (e.g., SIGMOD, VLDB, ICDE, SIGKDD, and SIGIR) must be very difficult for them to reach. They may have the following types of illusion.

(1) Those reviewers are god. They must understand everything we write in our paper. Moreover, they can immediately know the level of each paper.

(2) Those reviewers from top-tier venues must be very serious for reviewing every single word of the submitted papers. They will spend several days or weeks for reviewing them and spotting all weak parts. They can feel very angry (and have bad impression of us) if those papers are very incremental. Therefore, we need to make sure that (i) the idea is novel enough and (ii) every single word must be used perfectly before we start writing a paper. Otherwise, we will be blacklisted by those venues.

(3) Only those papers which have solid mathematical foundations and proofs (just like those papers from Albert Einstein) can be accepted in these venues.

(4) Every paper must change the world. Otherwise, it is not worth for publishing in a top-tier venue.

Fig. 2.11 Illusion from students for reviewers in top-tier venues (Part 1)

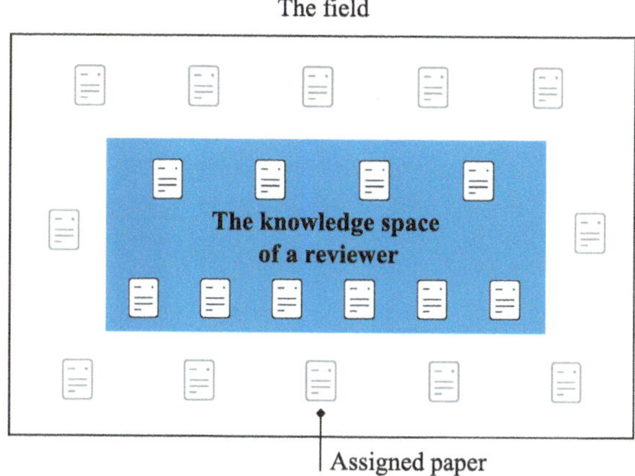

For (1), we would like to mention that reviewers are just humans but not god. They cannot understand everything in computer science. In addition, computer science can be deemed as one of the fastest changing subjects in the world. In 2021/2022, many researchers focused on computational epidemiology/blockchains/IoT. In 2022/2023, many researchers focused on ChatGPT/LLM. Now, many researchers further conduct research on the topics of AI for science and AI for everything. Since many new concepts can be established in just a few years, it is infeasible for everyone (even for top researchers) to follow the new research. Therefore, instead of thinking that they understand majority of research papers (see Fig. 2.11), we can assume that they only understand a limited amount of research papers (see Fig. 2.12).

For (2), we would like to mention that those reviewers in top-tier venues normally hold the faculty positions from universities. As a faculty in a university, we

Fig. 2.12 Reality of reviewers in top-tier venues (Part 1)

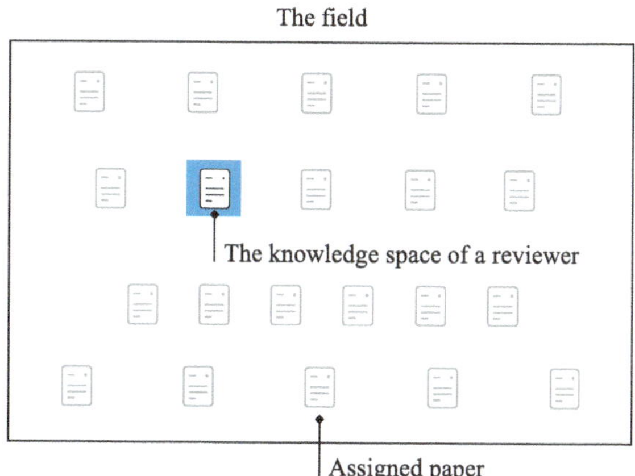

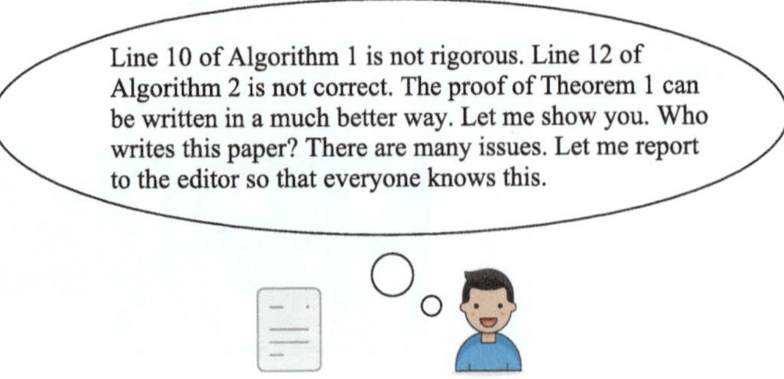

Fig. 2.13 Illusion from students for reviewers in top-tier venues (Part 2)

are extremely busy and need to handle many stuffs every day. We need to (i) submit many papers to a conference (help editing papers from students), (ii) prepare teaching materials/assignments/examination papers, (iii) attend dissertation defenses (of undergraduate students/master students/Ph.D. students), (iv) write proposals, (v) apply patents, (vi) attend academic conferences/activities, (vii) write books, (viii) handle administrative issues from departments/faculties/schools, (ix) have meetings with many people (e.g., students and other professors), (x) organize conferences (e.g., being a PC chair), (xi) review papers from various conferences/journals. Furthermore, reviewers also have their own family. They (especially for female) need to take care of their children and their father/mother. Therefore, it is nonsense to think that reviewers spend several days to review only your paper so that they can spot every error/issue from it (see Fig. 2.13). In addition, they will also have no time and no point to let other people know how bad your paper is (see Fig. 2.14). As such, unless there is an unethical issue (e.g., plagiarism) in your paper, you can feel free to submit it to a top-tier venue. Of course, we do not encourage you to submit something

Fig. 2.14 Reality of reviewers in top-tier venues (Part 2)

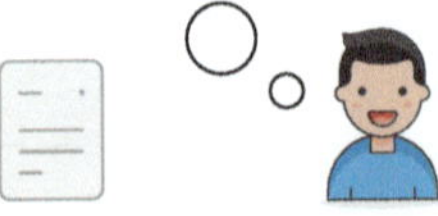

really bad, i.e., far below the threshold (e.g., an incomplete draft), to a top-tier venue. But as long as the draft is complete and the presentation flow is good, you should give a try.

For (3), many junior students may think that only those papers with solid theoretical foundations and proofs can arouse the interest from reviewers. Therefore, when some students see that their idea is not very mathematical, they will deliberately add some complicated equations/formulas in the paper with no sense. When you ask them the reasons for adding the (unrelated) equations, they will simply say that (i) the technical part is too simple and (ii) these equations look cool. To be honest, they are still too young if they really do something like this. A research paper is to convey scientific information between different scientists. Therefore, the most important part is to tell a good story and show how your idea can advance the state of the art. It is completely fine that a paper can have no equation if it can still be understood by others. Suppose that the technical part looks simple. What you need to do is to dig into the problem and conduct further research. If you really want to add an equation, you need to know the necessity of adding it (but not to say that it is cool).

For (4), many students may think that all papers in a top-tier venue must be the seminal papers, which will definitely change the world (see Fig. 2.15). However, this mindset is not correct. To be honest, majority of research papers in a top-tier venue are not very useful. Some of them even will not be mentioned in the future. Using the AAAI conference as an example, this conference accepts more than 1000 papers each year. Do you really think that 1000 seminal directions (like ChatGPT/Deepseek) can be established for one year? The answer is obviously no. Otherwise, we can achieve the goal of strong AI in a few years. Therefore, the ideas from most of these papers are in fact incremental, which only advance the field in a very limited way. However, the presentation of those papers must reach the level of a top-tier venue. As such, as long as the student has acquired the correct presentation skills, he/she can start writing papers (without being afraid of whether the idea is incremental). Some students may argue that these incremental papers are not worth for publications. Then, we will say

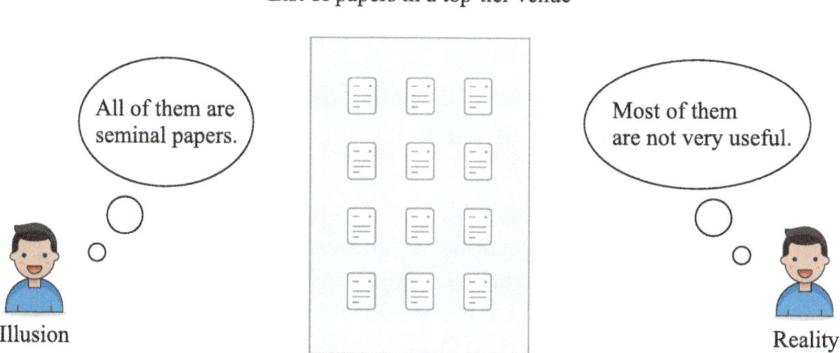

Fig. 2.15 Illusion and reality of papers in a top-tier venue

Fig. 2.16 A seminal paper is normally built on top of many incremental papers

that many seminal papers are built on top of those incremental papers (see Fig. 2.16). It is very hard for students to directly work on a seminal paper in the early stage since they do not acquire enough skills (especially for those junior students). Therefore, what they need to do is to work on some (probably incremental) research papers first (e.g., Paper 1 in Fig. 2.16). Based on the successful experience, they can explore more by asking more research questions. Ultimately, it is possible for students to achieve the impactful work. However, some students may still insist for working on seminal research without enough skills in the very early stage. Then, those students are hard to learn more skills (e.g., paper presentation skills, thinking skills), cannot even get one paper accepted (or even write a complete paper), and may be, unfortunately, kicked out from research labs.

2.7 Think That They Need to Hide Some Ideas for the Later Stage of Career

Many students may think that they will need to find the faculty positions in other universities. Therefore, they would like to hide some ideas so that they can publish them in the new positions (in order to make their CV better for tenure promotion). However, this mindset is only from a weak researcher (see Fig. 2.17). The main reason for a weak researcher to have this mindset is that he/she thinks that the topic space is similar to a ball with boundary. Once he/she has finished one topic, the space

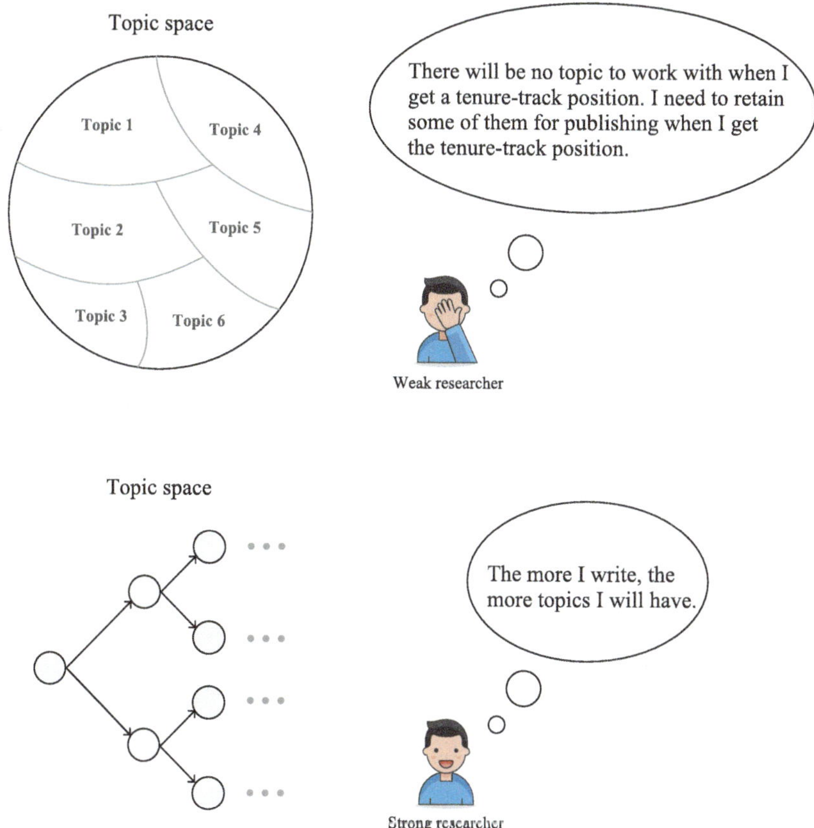

Fig. 2.17 Topic space (weak researcher vs. strong researcher)

is reduced. Therefore, he/she has the concern for whether all topics can be done so that he/she cannot have enough papers for tenure promotion in a new university.

However, if a student is well trained to be a strong (productive) researcher, he/she does not have this concern. The main reason is that he/she regards the topic space to be a tree structure with no boundary (see Fig. 2.17). As such, once he/she has written more papers, he/she can ask more questions, which correspond to different branches of the tree structure, in order to have more research topics in the future.

Hence, instead of worrying about the future tenure promotion, we strongly suggest that those weak researchers should improve their questioning skills. As an example, they should ask more research questions when they write each research paper. As another example, they should write more papers in order to practice these questioning skills (Practice makes perfect!). Once these skills are improved, they will not have this concern because they are no longer the weak researcher anymore.

2.8 Be Stubborn and Arrogant

Many students who would like to attend the postgraduate studies can normally have good academic records during the undergraduate studies (e.g., obtain high GPAs or get ACM competition awards). Therefore, some students may think that they are very good so that they refuse to listen to others (e.g., supervisors, postdoctoral researchers, and senior students). Consider the first author of this book as an example. He has some experiences for mentoring/supervising students. Here, we refer two students that were mentored/supervised by him to be "Student A" and "Student B" in the following discussion (due to the privacy issues). To his understanding, the student A initially had the better ability, including motivation, writing skills, and new methodology proposal skills, compared with the student B. However, the student A was very stubborn and arrogant, who could not accept any feedback from others and always thought that he is right. Comparatively, the student B lacked motivation but was willing to listen to his advices. At that time, he helped the student A edit research papers but the student A refused to adopt his version and told him that he did not work on the area of the student A before (so that he was not eligible to edit the paper from the student A) (see Fig. 2.18). Therefore, the student A insisted to

Fig. 2.18 A student who is stubborn and arrogant versus a student who is modest and listens to others

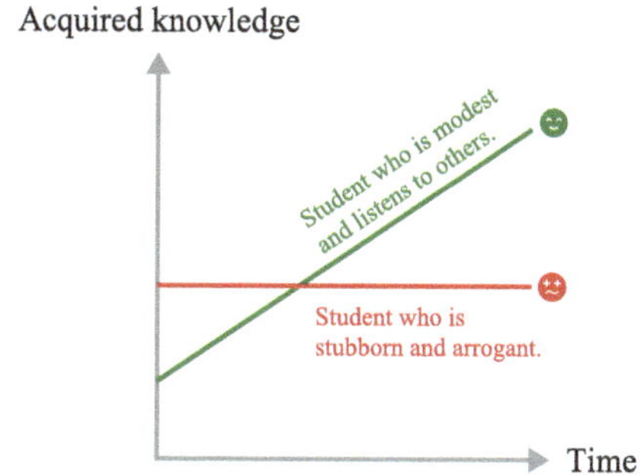

Fig. 2.19 Those students who are stubborn and arrogant cannot acquire knowledge

submit some unqualified (and unpolished) research papers to top-tier conferences, leading to rejection ultimately. On the other hand, he also edited the paper from the student B. Although he was not very happy regarding the motivation from the student B, this student listened carefully with his advices and allowed him to edit the paper (see Fig. 2.18). In the end, the student A did not get any paper accepted and the student B got one paper accepted in the top-tier venue. Moreover, during the mentoring/supervising process, he observed that the ability (knowledge) of the student B significantly increased while the ability of the student A remained the same (like Fig. 2.19).

Based on the above discussion, we emphasize that students (especially for junior students) need to be modest and listen to others, especially for some comments of writing. The main reason is that students can be regarded as newbies in research, who do not have solid experience for writing compared with faculty members/postdoctoral researchers. Without solid achievements (e.g., publishing a first-author paper in SIG-MOD, where only a few parts are edited by a mentor/supervisor), it is strongly encouraged for a student to listen to his/her mentor/supervisor.

2.9 Always Rely on Their Supervisors

In some research groups, the supervisors (especially for those young and energetic supervisors) may have a lot of research directions for students. Moreover, due to the tenure pressure, some supervisors can act as the "mother/father" and provide every step for their students to work on (Note that the number of successful student supervisions is an important indicator for whether a faculty member can be tenured.). Therefore, those students in the research group can simply wait for the next steps from their supervisors and can possibly have many top-tier publications (see Fig. 2.20). At that time, some students, who are from other research groups,

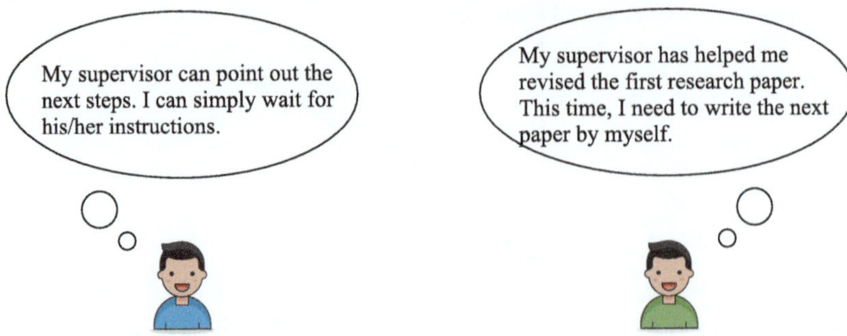

Fig. 2.20 Qualified research students need to learn how to conduct independent research during their postgraduate studies

may be envious of this. However, we would like to emphasize that this may not be a good thing since a qualified research student should not always be protected under the umbrella of his/her supervisor (see Fig. 2.20). In fact, we have seen that many students who have solid research achievements in the postgraduate studies can fail to maintain the productivity after graduation (see Fig. 2.21). The main reason is that these students still do not learn how to conduct independent research during their postgraduate studies. Therefore, the student, who wants to have the career path for

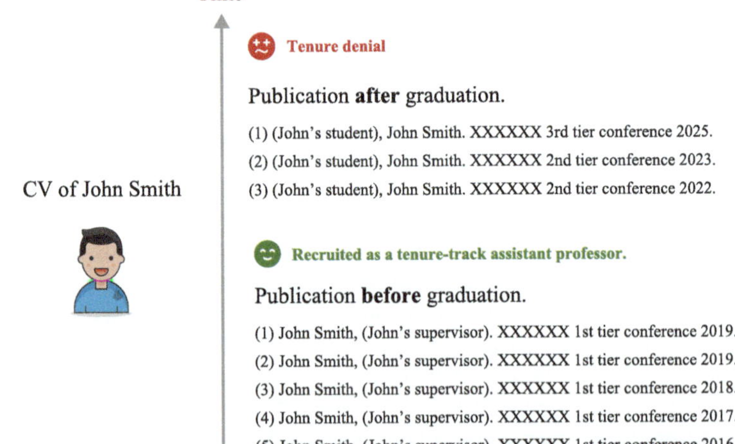

Fig. 2.21 Many productive research students cannot maintain the research productivity after graduation

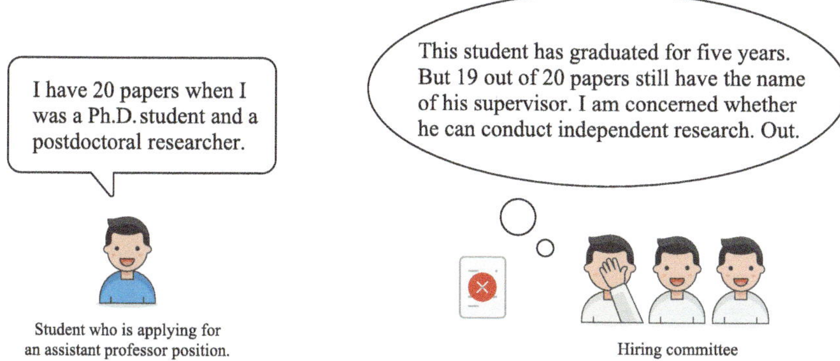

Fig. 2.22 A hiring committee of a faculty position will not hire someone who cannot demonstrate that he/she can conduct independent research

being a researcher in the future, should learn how to conduct independent research (though it can be painful in the first few papers). Once they have acquired the independent research skills and graduate, they should avoid having a lot of collaborations with their supervisors and try to establish collaborations with other professors in the communities. The two main reasons are that (1) they can learn different research styles from different researchers and (2) a hiring committee of a faculty member (e.g., an assistant professor position) only recruits someone who can demonstrate the independent research skills (see Fig. 2.22). Consider the first author of this book as an example. After he obtained the Ph.D. degree from the Hong Kong Polytechnic University (supervised by (Ken) Man Lung Yiu), he became a postdoctoral researcher in the University of Hong Kong (collaborated with Reynold Cheng) and a research assistant professor in the Hong Kong Baptist University (collaborated with Yun Peng, Byron Choi, and Jianliang Xu). With many collaboration and research experiences in different universities, he learned different styles and showed independent research skills (by reducing the number of publications with his Ph.D. supervisor, i.e., Ken Yiu). Observe from Fig. 2.23 that he, who graduated in March 2019, only had a small amount of representative research papers with his supervisor from 2021 to 2025 (mainly on or before 2022).

1.   Yue Zhong*, **Tsz Nam Chan**, Leong Hou U, Dingming Wu, Wei Tu, Ruisheng Wang, Joshua Zhexue Huang. "A Fast and Accurate Block Compression Solution for Spatiotemporal Kernel Density Visualization" **SIGKDD 2025** (To appear). **(CCF: A)**

2.   Siyue Wu, Dingming Wu, Sinhong Cheuk, **Tsz Nam Chan**, Kezhong Lu. "GREAT: Generalized Reservoir Sampling based Triangle Counting Estimation over Streaming Graphs" **PVLDB 2025** (To appear). **(CCF: A)**

3.   **Tsz Nam Chan**, Pak Lon Ip, Bojian Zhu, Leong Hou U, Dingming Wu, Jianliang Xu, Christian S. Jensen. "Large-scale Spatiotemporal Kernel Density Visualization" **ICDE 2025** (To appear). **(CCF: A)**

4.   Weike Tang, Dingming Wu, **Tsz Nam Chan**, Kezhong Lu: "Spatially Compact Dense Block Mining in Spatial Tensors" **SIGKDD 2025** (To appear). **(CCF: A)**

5.   Siyue Wu, Dingming Wu, Junyi Quan, **Tsz Nam Chan**, Kezhong Lu: "Efficient and Accurate PageRank Approximation on Large Graphs" **SIGMOD 2025** (To appear). **(CCF: A)**

6.   **Tsz Nam Chan**, Bojian Zhu, Dingming Wu, Yun Peng, Leong Hou U. "LARGE: A Length-Aggregation-based Grid Structure for Line Density Visualization" **PVLDB 2024** (vol 17) (To appear). **(CCF: A)**

7.   **Tsz Nam Chan**, Rui Zang, Bojian Zhu, Leong Hou U, Dingming Wu, Jianliang Xu. "LION: Fast and High-Resolution Network Kernel Density Visualization" **PVLDB 2024** (vol 17), pages 1255-1268. **(CCF: A)**

8.   Renchi Yang, Yidu Wu, Xiaoyang Lin, Qichen Wang, **Tsz Nam Chan**, Jieming Shi: "Effective Clustering on Large Attributed Bipartite Graphs" **SIGKDD 2024** (To appear). **(CCF: A)**

9.   Shunran Zhang, Xiubo Zhang, **Tsz Nam Chan**, Shenghui Zhang, Leong Hou U: "A Computation-aware Shape Loss Function for Point Cloud Completion" **AAAI 2024**, pages 7287-7295. **(CCF: A)**

10.   **Tsz Nam Chan**, Zhe Li, Leong Hou U, Reynold Cheng: "PLAME: Piecewise-Linear Approximate Measure for Additive Kernel SVM" **IEEE TKDE 2023** (vol 35) 9985-9997. **(CCF: A)**

11.   Yun Peng, Byron Choi, **Tsz Nam Chan**, Jianye Yang, Jianliang Xu: "Efficient Approximate Nearest Neighbor Search in Multi-dimensional Databases" **SIGMOD 2023** 1(1): 54:1-54:27. **(CCF: A)**

12.   **Tsz Nam Chan**, Leong Hou U, Byron Choi, Jianliang Xu: "SLAM: Efficient Sweep Line Algorithms for Kernel Density Visualization" **SIGMOD 2022**, pages 2120-2134. **(CCF: A)**

13.   **Tsz Nam Chan**, Leong Hou U, Yun Peng, Byron Choi, Jianliang Xu: "Fast Network K-function-based Spatial Analysis" **PVLDB 2022** (vol 15), pages 2853-2866. **(CCF: A)**

14.   **Tsz Nam Chan**, Pak Lon Ip, Leong Hou U, Byron Choi, Jianliang Xu: "SWS: A Complexity-Optimized Solution for Spatial-Temporal Kernel Density Visualization" **PVLDB 2022** (vol 15), pages 814-827. **(CCF: A)**

15.   **Tsz Nam Chan**, Pak Lon Ip, Leong Hou U, Byron Choi, Jianliang Xu: "SAFE: A Share-and-Aggregate Bandwidth Exploration Framework for Kernel Density Visualization" **PVLDB 2022** (vol 15), pages 513-526. **(CCF: A)**

16.   **Tsz Nam Chan**, Leong Hou U, Reynold Cheng, Man Lung Yiu, Shivansh Mittal: "Efficient Algorithms for Kernel Aggregation Queries" **IEEE TKDE 2022** (vol 34), pages 2726-2739. **(CCF: A)**

17.   Yun Peng, Byron Choi, **Tsz Nam Chan**, Jianliang Xu: "LAN: Learning-based Approximate k-Nearest Neighbor Search in Graph Databases" **ICDE 2022**, pages 2508-2521. **(CCF: A)**

18.   Zhe Li, Man Lung Yiu, **Tsz Nam Chan**: "PAW: Data Partitioning Meets Workload Variance" **ICDE 2022**, pages 123-135. **(CCF: A)**

19.   Zichen Zhu, **Tsz Nam Chan**, Reynold Cheng, Loc Do, Zhipeng Huang, Haoci Zhang: "Effective and Efficient Discovery of Top-k Meta Paths in Heterogeneous Information Networks" **IEEE TKDE 2022** (vol 34), pages 4172-4185. **(CCF: A)**

20.   Jie Chen, Zaifeng Yang, **Tsz Nam Chan**, Hui Li, Junhui Hou, Lap-Pui Chau: "Attention-Guided Progressive Neural Texture Fusion for High Dynamic Range Content Restoration" **IEEE TIP 2022** (vol 31), pages 2661-2672. **(CCF: A)**

21.   **Tsz Nam Chan**, Zhe Li, Leong Hou U, Jianliang Xu, Reynold Cheng: "Fast Augmentation Algorithms for Network Kernel Density Visualization" **PVLDB 2021** (vol 14), pages 1503-1516. **(CCF: A)**

22.   **Tsz Nam Chan**, Man Lung Yiu, Leong Hou U: "The Power of Bounds: Answering Approximate Earth Mover's Distance with Parametric Bounds" **IEEE TKDE 2021** (vol 33), pages 768-781. **(CCF: A)**

Fig. 2.23 Representative publications of Tsz Nam Chan from 2021 to 2025. Man Lung Yiu (covered by each red box) is his Ph.D. supervisor

Chapter 3
Common Mistakes and Correct Mindsets for Research Actions

In this chapter, we discuss some common mistakes regarding the research actions that have been taken by new postgraduate students (including us in the early stage of career), which can be categorized into nine types. We will also discuss the correct mindsets for the corresponding mistakes.

3.1 Solely Establish Foundations Based on Taking Courses

Once students transit from undergraduate studies to postgraduate studies, they still think that they can only master knowledge based on taking courses (see Fig. 3.1). Of course, taking courses (especially for some fundamental courses, e.g., advanced algorithm courses for some students who work on theory.) is still important. However, each course can be very broad, which covers a lot of topics. As an example, an advanced database course covers topics in relational databases (e.g., SQL, join, and relational algebra), spatial databases (e.g., R-tree), and graph databases (e.g., graph-based systems). Therefore, some students who mainly work on spatial databases can find that the knowledge in relational databases is not very useful/related to their research. Based on this, some productive students tend to master knowledge by reading research papers related to their research instead (see Fig. 3.1).

Some students may have an illusion that a Ph.D. should have mastered a broad range of knowledge. They have this illusion mainly because of some movies/TV series (e.g., Detective Galileo from Japan) or the interpretation from society. As such, these students may aim to master a broad range of knowledge during the postgraduate studies by taking courses. In fact, this mindset is incorrect. Those successful Ph.D. students (or faculty members) normally have a narrow set of knowledge (with very deep understanding). Using the first author of this book as an example, he is dedicated to research topics for developing efficient algorithms in GIS. Until now, he has only worked on "kernel density estimation", "K-function", and "line density estimation"

T. N. Chan and D. Wu, *Mastering the Academic Writing Mindset*,
https://doi.org/10.1007/978-981-95-4850-7_3

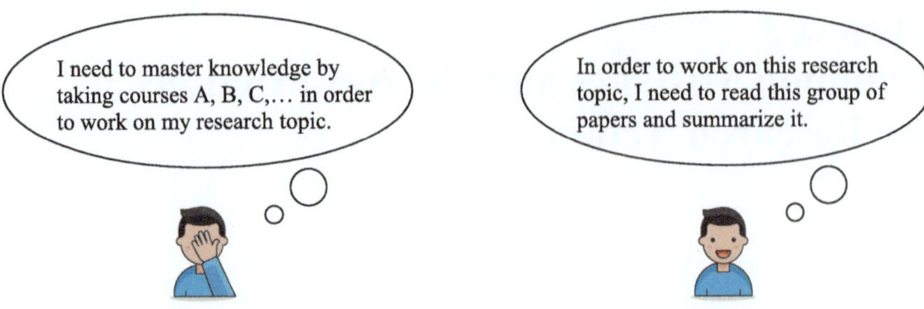

Fig. 3.1 Productive students master knowledge by reading research papers instead of taking a lot of courses

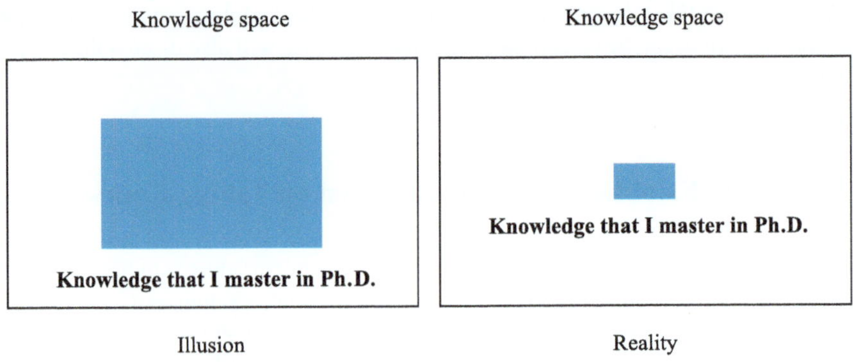

Fig. 3.2 Knowledge space: illusion versus reality

in GIS as a principal author. He has nearly zero knowledge for other research topics (e.g., neural networks). However, he received the title of National Science Fund for Excellent Young Scholars (Overseas), which is a prestigious title in China, with the age of 32, and has published nearly 20 research papers as a first author in top-tier database venues (including SIGMOD, VLDB, ICDE, and TKDE). Therefore, in reality, a Ph.D. should be regarded as "narrow but deep" instead of "broad but shallow" (see Fig. 3.2).

3.2　Never Care About Deadlines

Many students (especially for junior students) do not think that it is important to meet deadlines that they have mentioned before. When we ask them why they miss deadlines, they always have an excuse that they are busy with other things (see Fig. 3.3). However, they never try to meet what they have promised before.

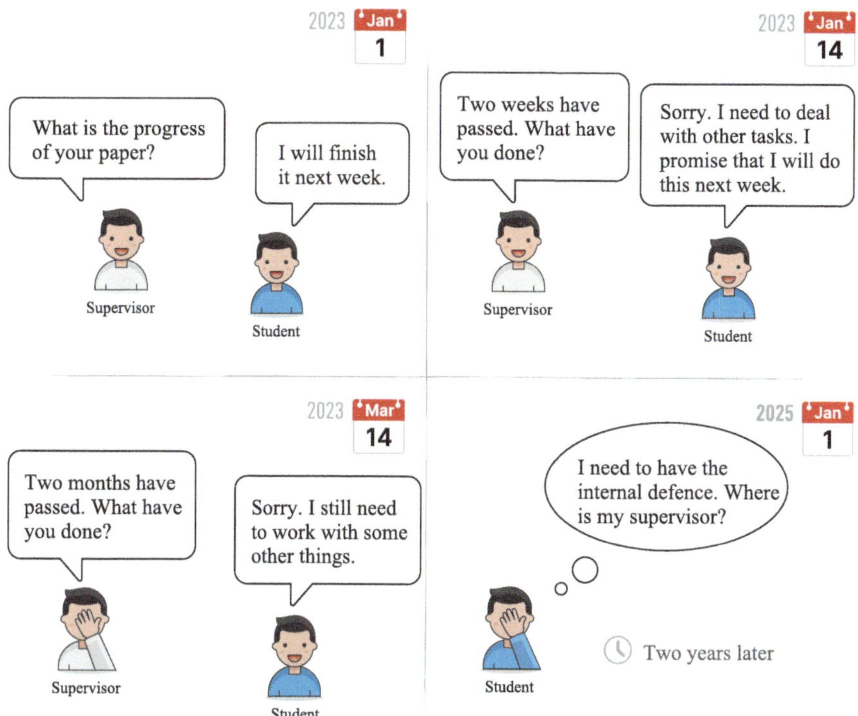

Fig. 3.3 An unproductive student always misses deadlines

For those students, we would like to say that the supervisors are not idiot. It is possible that you can miss the deadline for the first time. But if you keep missing the following deadlines, most of the supervisors can think that these students have no motivation for conducting research and start ignoring these lazy students. Some supervisors can even kick these students out of their research groups. In addition, it is easy for students to develop this kind of bad habit. The main reason is that a university is not the same as a company. There is no fixed working hours and clear tasks for them. The students can stay up late for playing computer games and drinking with their friends and come back to their offices at 5:00pm (without any idea for what to do next). In order to avoid developing this habit, the students need to have good time management. In other words, they need to have the quantitative goal every day in order to meet each deadline. For example, they can set the following reasonable goals.[1]

---

[1] As a remark, the goal must be reasonable. You should not set the goal for writing 100 pages in one day.

Fig. 3.4 A productive student can set a reasonable goal every day so that the supervisor does not set deadlines for him/her

(1) Write one to two paragraphs for the draft today.

(2) Implement the proposed method in these three days.

(3) Survey those papers from the area A and summarize them in the draft in the next two days.

By fulfilling the goal every day, it is likely for students to meet those deadlines (provided by their supervisors/other collaborators). Furthermore, students can find that they can develop the confidence for conducting research after they have always fulfilled these quantitative goals. With this good habit, the supervisor will not set any deadline for those students because they can conduct research independently (see Fig. 3.4).

3.3 Never Aim High for Submitting Papers

Many students may think that it is a painful experience for submitting papers to top-tier venues because of these three reasons. First, those papers are likely to be rejected since the acceptance rate of top-tier venues are normally lower than 25% (e.g., the

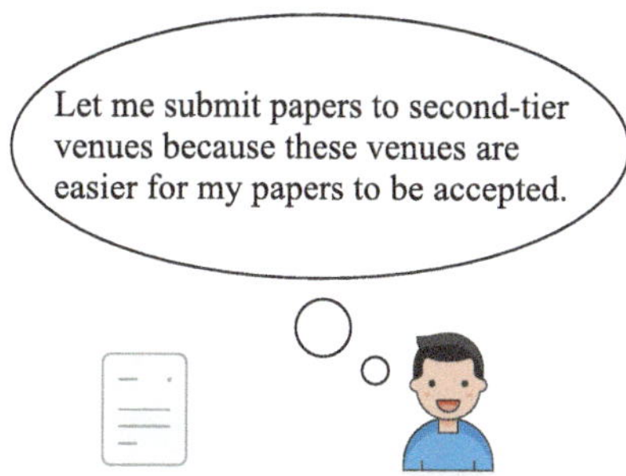

Ending: Most of the papers are either published in second-tier venues or third-tier venues. No prestigious university wants to hire him/her as an assistant professor.

Fig. 3.5 Students who do not aim high for submitting papers cannot have a good career

second round of SIGKDD 2025 only has the acceptance rate of 18.4%). Second, those authors are normally from top universities (e.g., UC Berkeley, MIT, Stanford, Technical University of Munich, Oxford, Tsinghua University, Peking University, NUS, KAIST, and University of Tokyo) in the world. Third, many harsh comments are received by the authors for each submission, which are very hard to be addressed. Therefore, they may only aim to submit papers to some second-tier (or even third-tier) venues (see Fig. 3.5), which should be an easy path for them. Indeed, those second-tier venues can let students have the happy life during their postgraduate studies. However, these second-tier venues are hard for helping students increase their research and presentation skills. Here, we consider this analogy. Imagine that you are playing an online game. If you only fight for those monsters with low levels (e.g., level 1 to level 5), it is hard for you to increase your level. In order to significantly increase your level, what you need to do is to kill those monsters with higher levels (e.g., level 10 and level 20) for earning more experience. As such, suppose that you have a lot of second-tier or even third-tier publications. The hiring committee for an assistant professor in a university will seriously doubt whether this student has enough ability to conduct high-quality research in the future. We can guarantee that those prestigious universities have zero chance to hire anyone who has many weak publications.

Consider those students who only submit papers to top-tier venues (see Fig. 3.6). Indeed, this can be a painful experience because those papers can possibly be rejected for several times. However, those students can learn the high-quality research and presentation skills based on those comments. Moreover, they can significantly increase their ability (by obtaining more experience) during the submission/rejection process. Ultimately, they can have enough ability to independently submit their own research papers and make them accepted to these top-tier venues. With many top-tier publications (i.e., solid research background), it is easy for them to get the offers from prestigious universities (or top research labs/research-based companies).

Ending: He/she may get frustrated in the first few papers but he/she gains a lot of experience (learns the presentation) during these submissions. He/she can independently submit his/her own papers in top-tier venues. Many prestigious universities want to hire him/her after graduation.

Fig. 3.6 Students who aim high for submitting papers can have a good career

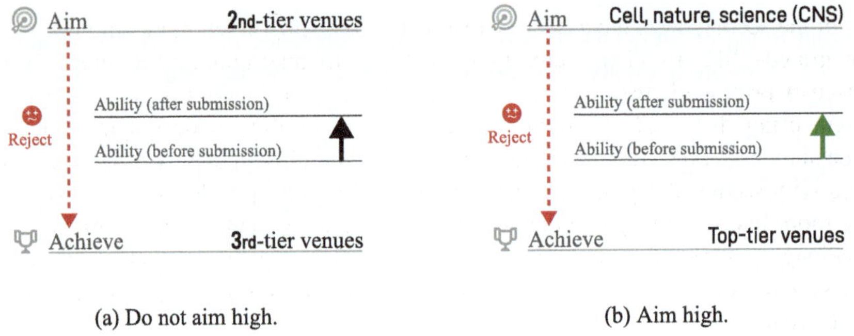

(a) Do not aim high.   (b) Aim high.

Fig. 3.7 An additional reason for why we need to aim high for submitting papers

Figure 3.7 further mentions the additional reason for why we need to aim high for submitting papers. Suppose that we target for the most difficult and the best venues (e.g., cell, nature, and science (CNS)). Even though those papers are rejected (i.e., failure), it is likely that we can still make them published in some top-tier venues. However, if we only target for the second-tier venues, it is likely that the paper will ultimately be published in the third-tier venues (after the rejection). Moreover, like what we mentioned before, targeting for the best venues can help us increase the ability so that it can increase our chance for making the papers accepted for those venues next time. If we only submit papers to some second-tier venues, we will no longer have the chance to get papers accepted in the best venues.

3.4 Select a Research Topic That They Are Not Interested in

Nowadays, many students would like to work on those research topics that are very trendy (see Fig. 3.8), e.g., artificial intelligence (AI), computer vision (CV), natural language processing (NLP), deep learning (DL), and large language models (LLM). However, most of these students do not have any background (i.e., prior knowledge) about these topics. Worse still, some of these students may even do not like these topics. The main reason for why they want to work on these topics is that many companies (e.g., Tencent AI, Alibaba, Huawei, Google Brain, and Amazon) may have the higher chance for providing high salary to hire someone with these backgrounds. Here, we need to emphasize that this mindset is completely wrong based on the following reasons.

Reason 1 (It is impossible to determine whether your research topic is still hot when you graduate.): Observe from Fig. 3.9 that a research topic must not be hot forever. Even though a research topic is hot when you start your postgraduate study, it is possible that this topic will not be hot when you graduate. Consider the experience

Fig. 3.8 A research topic may not be job-oriented. But it must be something that you really enjoy for

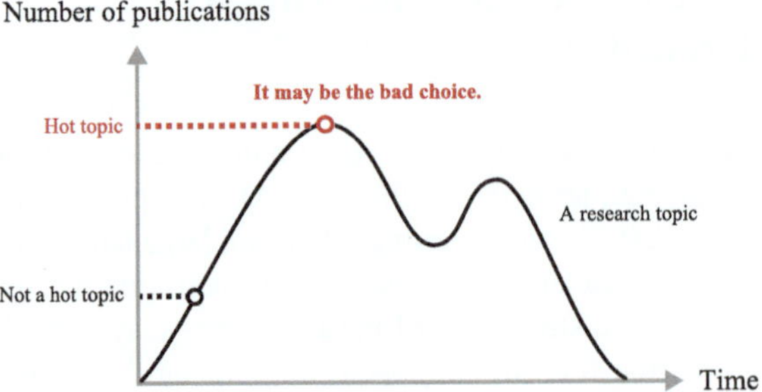

Fig. 3.9 A research topic is not hot forever (especially for computer science, which is a fast growing field)

of the first author of this book as an example. When he started his Ph.D. study in 2014, the hot topic in the database community was crowdsourcing (i.e., leveraging a group of people to work on a single task while minimizing the cost). However, this topic was not hot anymore when it was in 2018 (the time when he submitted the Ph.D. thesis). Therefore, suppose that some students only want to work on a hot topic that is not their interest and think that it can help them find a good job. It is possible that they will ultimately be very disappointed as they may find that it is hard for them to publish any paper (because they do not like that topic) and they may not find a good job (as the topic may not be hot anymore).

Reason 2 (Even though a research area is hot, it does not mean a company needs to hire you.): Suppose that you are lucky and your research topic is still hot when you graduate. It does not mean that it is easy for you to get a job in a company. The main reason is that many students may also work on this topic at the same time (see Fig. 3.10), indicating that there are many competitors for an offer in a company. Even

Fig. 3.10 Working on a hot topic does not guarantee that you must get an offer of a job

Fig. 3.11   Working on a topic that is not hot does not guarantee that you cannot get an offer of a job

though you work on a research topic that is not hot, it does not mean that you cannot get a job offer. Instead, it is possible for you to easily get an offer because not many people work on this topic, which means you have nearly no competitor for an offer (see Fig. 3.11).

Reason 3 (It is extremely hard for you to produce anything if you do not like it.): When you were young, you had different interests, e.g., playing computer games, playing football, and chatting with friends. At that time, you did these tasks without being told by your mother and your father. The main reason is that you are interested in these tasks. Therefore, you did them even though no one told you to do so. Note

Fig. 3.12   Interest is the best teacher

that this is the same as conducting research (see Fig. 3.12). If you are interested in one research topic, you will automatically plan for the next tasks and keep having progress. However, if you are not interested in that topic, you may not be motivated to work on it. You may somehow just want to "fulfill" the tasks from your supervisor (see Sect. 2.1). Therefore, you need to keep asking yourself this question. **Which research topic are you really interested in?** By answering this question, you should expect that you need to be fully dedicated into this research topic for the next four years.

3.5 Do Nothing During the Idle Time

We believe that many (junior) students may have this experience before. When they need to wait for somethings (e.g., the experimental results, the draft which is currently edited by supervisors, and the information from the collaborators), they will not do anything that can push the progress of the paper (see Fig. 3.13). Consider the first author of this book as an example. In the early stage of his postgraduate study (from September 2014 to January 2017), he simply sat in front of the monitor and waited for the experimental results after he had implemented each method. He did not know what he should do next during the idle time in order to further improve the research paper. Therefore, he was not very productive in that time period. Hence, we need to emphasize that those productive students do not waste their idle time (see Fig. 3.13).

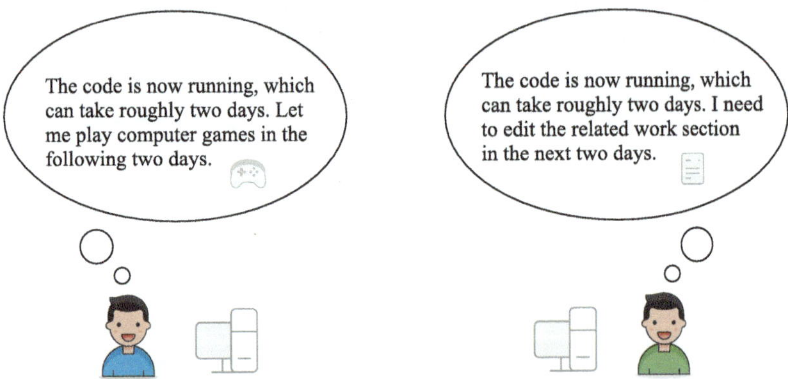

Ending: This student is not productive during his/her postgraduate study.

Ending: This student is very productive during his/her postgraduate study.

Fig. 3.13 Productive students do not waste their idle time

3.6 Have No Plan for What to Do Ahead

Many junior students have no (concrete) plan for what to do ahead (see Fig. 3.14). Without the plan, it is easy for students to get lost every day. When they sit down in front of the monitor and turn on the computer, they will have nothing to start. Therefore, it is easy for these students to surf the internet for doing nothing related to research (e.g., checking the emails, checking the news, and playing the online games). Ultimately, they will find that they have done nothing (or have only a few progress) for each day. The main reason is that students who want to be successful need to set the concrete goals (e.g., finish the kernel density visualization topic before 30th June 2021). With these goals, they can set the plans for achieving them. Once the students have their plans, they can automatically know what they should do when they go to their offices. Here, we emphasize that only those students (with clear plans) can be productive and have potential to be a successful faculty member (see Fig. 3.14).

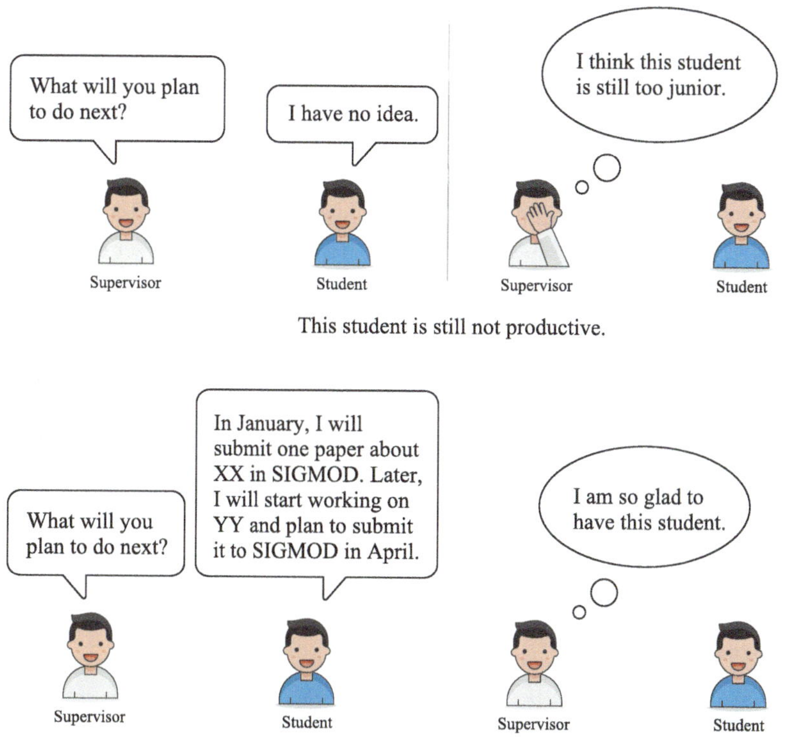

Fig. 3.14 An unproductive student has no plan for what to do next while a productive student plans for several paper submissions ahead

3.7 Only Want to Find Internships During the Postgraduate Studies

Many students may not want to be fully dedicated to conduct research during their postgraduate studies. Instead, they only want to find internships, which may even not be related to their research, for earning money or working experience. All they want to get is simply a postgraduate degree certificate so that many companies are willing to recruit them with high salaries (see Fig. 3.15). For those students, we would like to emphasize the following three points.

Those students do not need this degree. Note that a postgraduate degree (excluding a taught postgraduate degree) is mainly for students to conduct research, write research papers, and present research work. These students will be trained in a way that they can have enough ability to work in a university, a research lab, and a research company. Suppose that those students only want to find internships that are not related to their research. It is not meaningful for them to get this degree for staying in academia. Instead, they can find a full-time job, which has a much higher

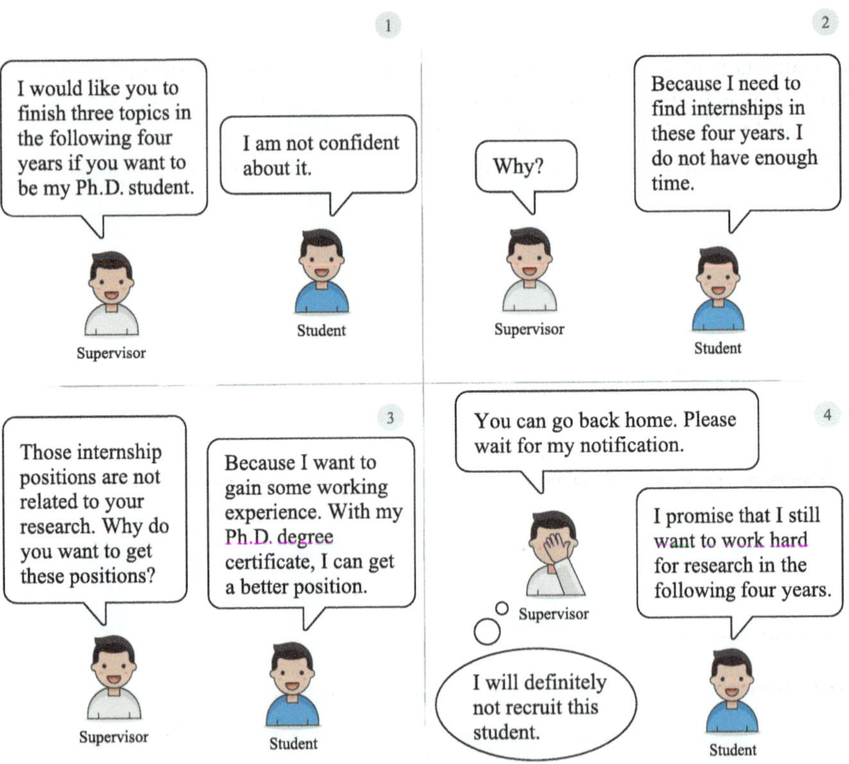

Fig. 3.15 Some students only want to find internships during the postgraduate studies

salary compared with the one of an internship position. Some students may have the false hope that this certificate can allow them to get a decent job in a top research lab (e.g., Tencent AI and Microsoft Research). However, these research labs only recruit those students who have solid research outcomes. With this bad attitude, we believe that these students may not have enough top-tier research publications for those labs to consider.

Those students will be very painful during the postgraduate studies. Since those students may not be willing to conduct research, they will not enjoy what they work on (e.g., reading papers, writing drafts, and thinking new solutions) every day. They may find some excuses to avoid the tasks assigned by their supervisors or may simply "fulfill" the tasks by their supervisors (see Sect. 2.1). Therefore, their supervisors may feel extremely angry about their progress and regularly blame them. Furthermore, once the graduation date is close, they will be anxious about their theses because they have not done anything.

The supervisors will not let those students graduate if they do not have enough research outcomes. Many supervisors normally have their requirements for graduation. Using Ph.D. students as an example, they normally need to finish three research topics in four years in order to write a Ph.D. thesis for graduation. Suppose that the students have no faith to conduct research. They may not be able to write one research paper, not to mention three research papers. As such, these students may ultimately need to defer their graduations, causing anxiety and losing the precious time for earning money and working experience.

3.8 Stick to the Same Problem Setting as a Previous Paper

Many postgraduate students may think that their new research papers must follow exactly the same problem setting as a previous paper in order to make sure that they do not solve the "wrong" problem (i.e., do the "real" stuff). They have this mindset mainly because of the following reasons.

They are afraid to motivate a new problem setting. Some junior students may not have enough writing skills/background knowledge. Therefore, they are afraid to write the abstract/introduction for discussing the background of the problem setting (see Fig. 3.16). Therefore, these students may choose the "safe" route by simply following exactly the same problem setting as the previous paper. The main reason is that they think that they can somehow "copy" the introduction from these papers so that they do not need to "write" the introduction.

They do not understand the background of that problem well enough. Some students may not understand the background of their research problems well enough. Consider the first author of this book as an example. When he was a junior Ph.D. student (roughly from 2014 to 2015), he worked on a fundamental research topic in image processing, called template matching. Note that this operation aims to find

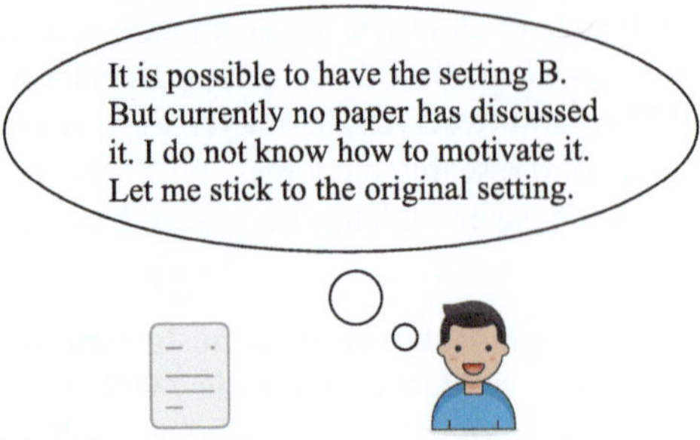

Fig. 3.16 A student can be afraid to motivate a new research problem

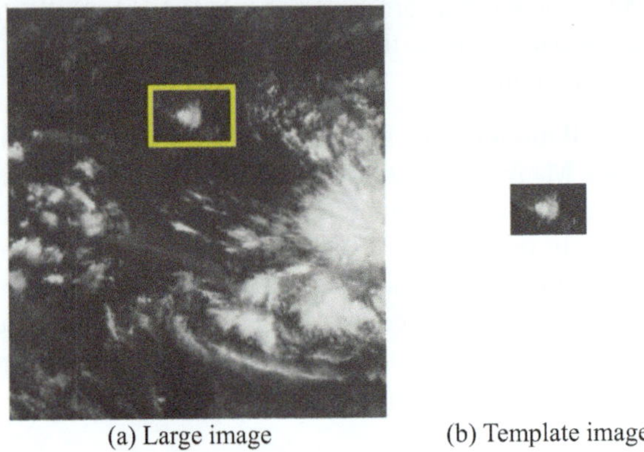

(a) Large image   (b) Template image

Fig. 3.17 Illustration of the template matching problem, where the image patch covered by the yellow box is the closest one to the template image. (Obtained from Fig. 1a and Fig. 1b in "Tsz Nam Chan, Man Lung Yiu, Kien A. Hua. Efficient Sub-Window Nearest Neighbor Search on Matrix. IEEE TKDE 2017")

the image patch from a large image that is the closest to a given template image (see Fig. 3.17). Due to the efficiency issues mentioned by many image processing/pattern recognition papers, he followed exactly the same problem setting and focused on developing efficient algorithms for this operation. However, the main reason for why he sticked to this problem setting is that he did not understand the background for why users need to adopt this operation. Moreover, he also did not acquire enough writing skills for motivating new settings of this problem.

They think that solving the same problem setting can advance the state of the art. Some junior students may think that publishing a paper is similar to a competition/an examination, which means that the problem setting must be the same and they need to develop the best solution that can achieve the state-of-the-art performance in order to publish a research paper.

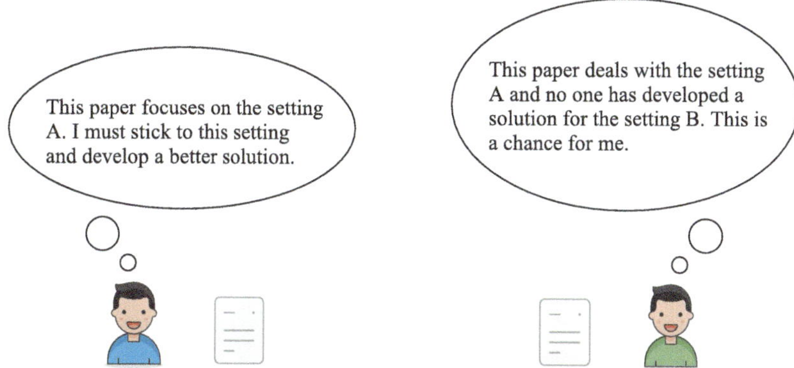

Ending: It is very hard for this student to figure out the new solution.

Ending: It is easy for this student to develop a new solution.

Fig. 3.18   It is relatively easy for students to produce results for a new problem setting

For the above students, we would like to emphasize that their mindsets may be wrong due to the following reasons.[2]

Easy to produce results for new problem settings. Note that those research problem settings that have been done by other researchers are hard for students to further develop a new solution for improving the performance. Instead, the new research problem settings can be easy for students to produce results (see Fig. 3.18). The main reason is that other researchers may have already developed strong solutions, which can be much better than the naïve one. Therefore, it is quite hard to develop another solution that can be much better than the existing solutions, i.e., only a small room (or even no room) for improvement (see Fig. 3.19).

Relatively hard to make papers accepted with the same problem setting.   Even though a student can manage to submit the paper with the same problem setting as the previous paper, it also has the high chance for the reviewer who published that previous paper to review the paper from the student. Normally, if the reviewer is very familiar with that topic, he/she can possibly be very harsh to the paper. The main reason is that the reviewer can easily detect any mistakes/flaws (even for very tiny ones) in the paper. Moreover, as the reviewer is the real expert for that research problem, he/she can, unfortunately, have the very high expectation for the methodology part. Therefore, he/she can easily reject the paper based on the technical novelty/contribution issues (see Fig. 3.20).

---

[2] For those students who are ambitious to work on fundamental problems with rich experience (e.g., developing new algorithms for further reducing the worst case time complexity to solve the matrix multiplication problem), the following reasons do not apply to them.

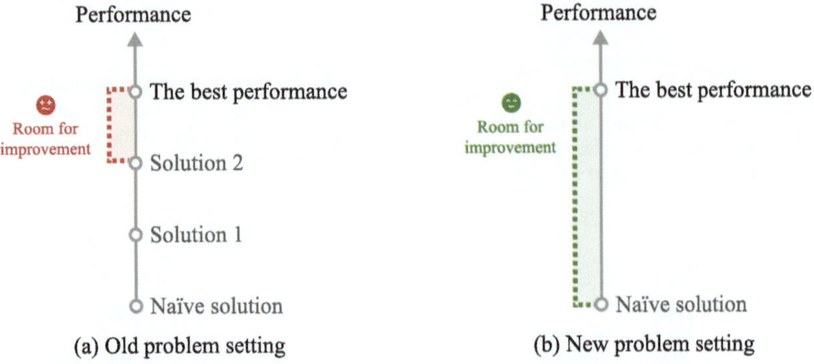

Fig. 3.19 Room for improvement (old problem setting vs. new problem setting)

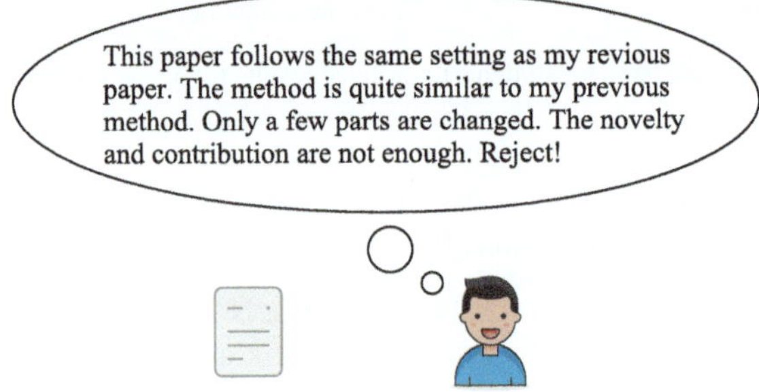

Fig. 3.20 The submitted paper can be easily assigned to and rejected by the reviewer who published the paper with the same problem setting before

3.9 Avoid Attending Academic Conferences

Many students may think that conducting research is to stay in the office (or in the library), think of big research ideas, and do not need to attend any social activities (e.g., academic conferences). They have this mindset mainly because the society (or some TV shows) may depict that scientists/researchers do not have good social skills (e.g., only stay in a room and think of a lot of ideas). However, this mindset is incorrect, which is based on the following reasons.

Human beings are gregarious. Therefore, all of us should enjoy social activities rather than staying alone for a long time. This is why it is nonsense to say that scientists/researchers, who are also humans, do not love social events. Moreover, it is even more nonsense to say that scientists/researchers should have bad social skills in order to be "qualified" scientists/researchers. Academic conferences should be the way for many researchers from worldwide to connect with each other, which should be regarded as happy and important events for scientists/researchers to attend (but not a waste of time). In addition, there are also three important reasons for why we need to attend academic conferences.

Many new ideas can be obtained by attending conferences. Consider the first author of this book as an example. He attended the SIGMOD 2017 conference, which was held in Chicago in May 2017. At that time, he listened to a paper presentation, called "Scalable Kernel Density Classification via Threshold-Based Pruning". That paper arouses the interest from him during the conference. Moreover, this presentation let him know that (1) kernel-based statistical models are computationally expensive, (2) improving the efficiency of kernel density estimation model is an important direction, and (3) this direction is very interesting. As such, he immediately started this research topic on September 2017 and published the ICDE 2019 paper related to this topic.

- **Tsz Nam Chan**, Man Lung Yiu, Leong Hou U. KARL: Fast Kernel Aggregation Queries. **ICDE 2019**.

With this paper, he further successfully published a lot of papers regarding how to improve the efficiency of handling kernel-based machine learning models and kernel density visualization. Therefore, without attending this conference, he may take a longer time to (or even may not be able to) figure out this topic, which can slow down his research progress (or even lose a lot of research papers).

Many research collaborations can be established during the academic conferences. Using the first author of this book as an example, the first time for him to meet with his collaborator Ryan Leong Hou U, who is a faculty member in University of Macau, was in the SIGMOD 2017 conference (Until now, they have more than 20 publications in prestigious venues.). At that time, they discussed the paper about how to improve the efficiency of computing Earth Mover's Distance (the first paper collaborated by them together) and that paper was later accepted in the TKDE journal.

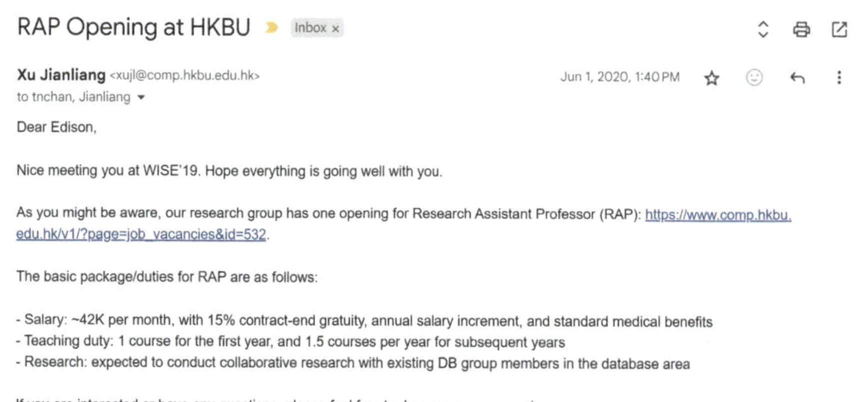

Fig. 3.21 The first author of this book obtains the job opportunity with the title of "Research Assistant Professor" in the Hong Kong Baptist University (HKBU) after attending the WISE 2019 conference

Many job opportunities can possibly be available during the academic conferences. Note that many research-based companies, e.g., Huawei, Tencent, Alibaba, Google, and Microsoft, have their counters for some academic conferences. Therefore, some students can utilize this chance to find some internship positions (or even full-time positions after graduation). Moreover, some senior professors may also want to recruit junior researchers (e.g., senior postgraduate students and postdoctoral researchers) into their universities. Therefore, those junior researchers can also make use of this chance to meet with many professors there in order to find faculty positions. Here, we consider the first author of this book as an example. In the early 2020, he was appointed to be the helper in the WISE 2019 conference (this conference is delayed to the early 2020 due to the serious protest in Hong Kong after June 2019). At that time, he met with a full professor (now a chair professor), called Jianliang Xu, in the Hong Kong Baptist University (HKBU). During the discussion in the conference, Jianliang knew that he would like to find a faculty position. As such, Jianliang sent an email on 1st June 2020 to invite him for joining HKBU as a research assistant professor (see Fig. 3.21). Later, he officially joined HKBU on 1st September 2020 and significantly increased his research productivity for the later three years (from 1st September 2020 to 31st August 2023) in HKBU.

Chapter 4
Common Mistakes and Correct Mindsets
for Reading and Writing Attitudes

In this chapter, we discuss some common mistakes for reading and writing attitudes that have been made by new postgraduate students (including us in the early stage of career), which have been categorized into the following fifteen types.

4.1 Accept Everything They Read in a Published Paper

Since the undergraduate study in computer science and its related fields is mainly course-based, the contents of those course materials/textbooks are normally correct. The main reason is that those knowledges have been well established/tested in several decades. As an example, Dijkstra's shortest path algorithm, which is taught in Algorithm courses, was developed in 1957. This algorithm has been used for more than 60 years, which is already a de facto standard. Therefore, the undergraduate students usually regard everything that they read to be the truth. What they need to do is to memorize those materials and to understand the mechanism behind those algorithms/frameworks/concepts in order to get a high grade in each course. They seldom raise some questions (or doubts) about the contents of those course materials/textbooks because these actions cannot help them get the high grades. However, some students (especially for those with high grades) may transfer these mindsets for the postgraduate studies. They may accept everything they read in a research paper, regard it as the truth, and do not raise any question about it. Note that this mindset is **completely wrong** in postgraduate studies. Here, we use an example for illustrating why it is wrong.

Example: In 2019, the first author of this book worked on a problem called kernel density visualization (KDV), which is used to generate a hotspot map based on some location data points (see Fig. 4.1). He developed efficient algorithms for generating an approximate KDV since the time complexity of this operation is very high, which takes $O(XYn)$ time (where $X \times Y$ and n denote the resolution size and the number

© The Author(s) 2026

T. N. Chan and D. Wu, *Mastering the Academic Writing Mindset*,

https://doi.org/10.1007/978-981-95-4850-7_4

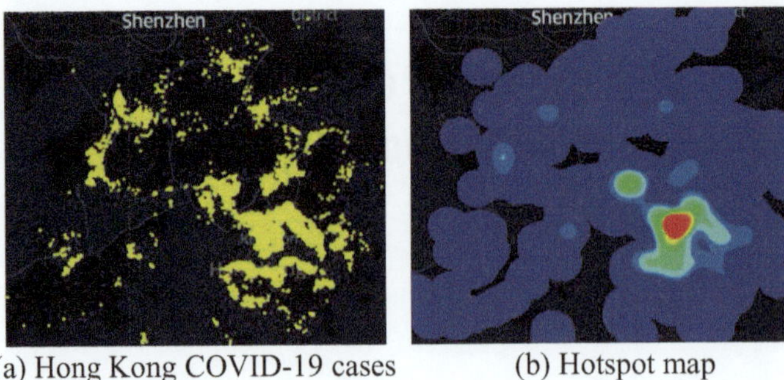

(a) Hong Kong COVID-19 cases   (b) Hotspot map

Fig. 4.1 Generating a hotspot map (based on KDV) for the Hong Kong COVID-19 location dataset. (Obtained from Fig. 1 in "Tsz Nam Chan, Leong Hou U, Byron Choi, Jianliang Xu, Reynold Cheng. Large-scale Geospatial Analytics: Problems, Challenges, and Opportunities. SIGMOD Conference Companion 2023")

of location data points, respectively). This work has been published in SIGMOD 2020, which is stated below.

- **Tsz Nam Chan**, Reynold Cheng, Man Lung Yiu. QUAD: Quadratic-Bound-based Kernel Density Visualization. **SIGMOD 2020**.

Suppose that a MPhil/Ph.D. supervisor assigns this topic for the student to follow up and the student still adopts the mindset for accepting everything he/she reads in a published paper. This student will immediately give up this topic when he/she reads the abstract of this paper (see Fig. 4.2). The most "proper reason" from this student is that this method can already achieve the real-time performance (0.5 s) for generating KDV under a single machine setting (underlined in red in the abstract), which is too good and there will be no room for improvement (i.e., don't waste time for investigating this topic). If it were really true, the following list of further research studies, which are all in top-tier database and data mining venues (SIGMOD, SIGKDD, VLDB, and ICDE), will no longer appear.

- **Tsz Nam Chan**, Zhe Li, Leong Hou U, Jianliang Xu, Reynold Cheng. Fast Augmentation Algorithms for Network Kernel Density Visualization. **VLDB 2021**.
- **Tsz Nam Chan**, Pak Lon Ip, Leong Hou U, Weng Hou Tong, Shivansh Mittal, Ye Li, Reynold Cheng. KDV-Explorer: A Near Real-Time Kernel Density Visualization System for Spatial Analysis. **VLDB 2021**. (Demo track)
- **Tsz Nam Chan**, Leong Hou U, Byron Choi, Jianliang Xu. SLAM: Efficient Sweep Line Algorithms for Kernel Density Visualization. **SIGMOD 2022**.
- **Tsz Nam Chan**, Pak Lon Ip, Leong Hou U, Byron Choi, Jianliang Xu. SAFE: A Share-and-Aggregate Bandwidth Exploration Framework for Kernel Density Visualization. **VLDB 2022**.
- **Tsz Nam Chan**, Pak Lon Ip, Leong Hou U, Byron Choi, Jianliang Xu. SWS: A Complexity-Optimized Solution for Spatial-Temporal Kernel Density Visualization. **VLDB 2022**.

Fig. 4.2 The abstract of the SIGMOD 2020 paper. (Obtained from "Tsz Nam Chan, Reynold Cheng, Man Lung Yiu. QUAD: Quadratic-Bound-based Kernel Density Visualization. SIGMOD 2020")

ABSTRACT

Kernel density visualization, or KDV, is used to view and understand data points in various domains, including traffic or crime hotspot detection, ecological modeling, chemical geology, and physical modeling. Existing solutions, which are based on computing kernel density (KDE) functions, are computationally expensive. Our goal is to improve the performance of KDV, in order to support large datasets (e.g., one million points) and high screen resolutions (e.g., 1280×960 pixels). We examine two widely-used variants of KDV, namely approximate kernel density visualization (ϵKDV) and thresholded kernel density visualization (τKDV). For these two operations, we develop fast solution, called QUAD, by deriving quadratic bounds of KDE functions for different types of kernel functions, including Gaussian, triangular etc. We further adopt a progressive visualization framework for KDV, in order to stream partial visualization results to users continuously. Extensive experiment results show that our new KDV techniques can provide at least one-order-of-magnitude speedup over existing methods, without degrading visualization quality. We further show that QUAD can produce the reasonable visualization results in real-time (0.5 sec) by combining the progressive visualization framework in single machine setting without using GPU and parallel computation.

- **Tsz Nam Chan**, Pak Lon Ip, Kaiyan Zhao, Leong Hou U, Byron Choi, Jianliang Xu. LIBKDV: A Versatile Kernel Density Visualization Library for Geospatial Analytics. **VLDB 2022**. (Demo track)
- **Tsz Nam Chan**, Leong Hou U, Byron Choi, Jianliang Xu, Reynold Cheng. Large-scale Geospatial Analytics: Problems, Challenges, and Opportunities. **SIGMOD 2023**. (Tutorial track)
- **Tsz Nam Chan**, Rui Zang, Pak Lon Ip, Leong Hou U, Jianliang Xu. PyNKDV: An Efficient Network Kernel Density Visualization Library for Geospatial Analytic Systems. **SIGMOD 2023**. (Demo track)
- **Tsz Nam Chan**, Rui Zang, Bojian Zhu, Leong Hou U, **Dingming Wu**, Jianliang Xu. LION: Fast and High-Resolution Network Kernel Density Visualization. **VLDB 2024**.
- **Tsz Nam Chan**, Pak Lon Ip, Bojian Zhu, Leong Hou U, **Dingming Wu**, Jianliang Xu, Christian S. Jensen. Large-scale Spatiotemporal Kernel Density Visualization. **ICDE 2025**.
- Yue Zhong, **Tsz Nam Chan**, Leong Hou U, **Dingming Wu**, Wei Tu, Ruisheng Wang, Joshua Zhexue Huang. A Fast and Accurate Block Compression Solution for Spatiotemporal Kernel Density Visualization. **SIGKDD 2025**.

Therefore, we can observe that this student may give up the chance for establishing a new field and give up a lot of top-tier publications if he/she adopts the wrong mindset

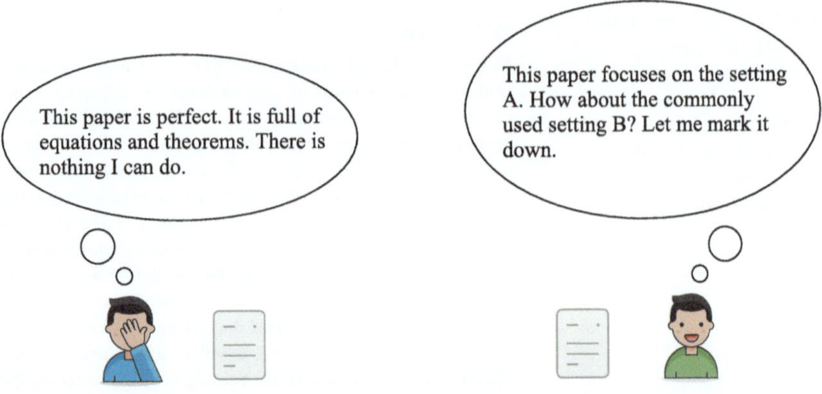

Fig. 4.3 Unproductive students do not ask questions when they read papers, while productive students ask questions and mark down many new directions when they read papers

by accepting everything he/she reads in a published paper. Here, we would like to emphasize that many authors would like to use the style of "selling the good things and hiding the bad things" for writing papers. The main reason is that this approach easily makes reviewers feel impressed so that they can give an "Accept" for their papers. As such, the readers need to ask questions/raise doubts about what they read instead of accepting everything. **Asking questions (see Fig.** 4.3) **is the only way to (1) figure out the weakness of the paper and (2) identify the new research directions.**

4.2 Read Every Paper Line-By-Line

When the students are in the undergraduate studies, they need to read the course materials (or probably textbooks) from cover to cover in order to grasp all those concepts so that they can get an A+/A grade in each course. These students may keep the habit and read every paper line-by-line and cover to cover. They may think that this can help them understand the paper thoroughly. However, this mindset is not correct, which is not realistic and feasible for obtaining/understanding knowledge nowadays. In recent years, gradually more papers are submitted to top-tier conferences/journals. Consider several top-tier AI/ML conferences in 2024, including IJCAI, AAAI, ICML, and NeurIPS. Each conference accepts more than 1000 papers in that year. Using Fig. 4.4 as an example, the number of pages of the last paper in AAAI 2024 has already reached 23,861. Some database conferences, which have relatively smaller numbers of papers for each year, also contain more than 200 publications per year. As an example, the number of research papers that are presented in VLDB 2024 is more than 250.

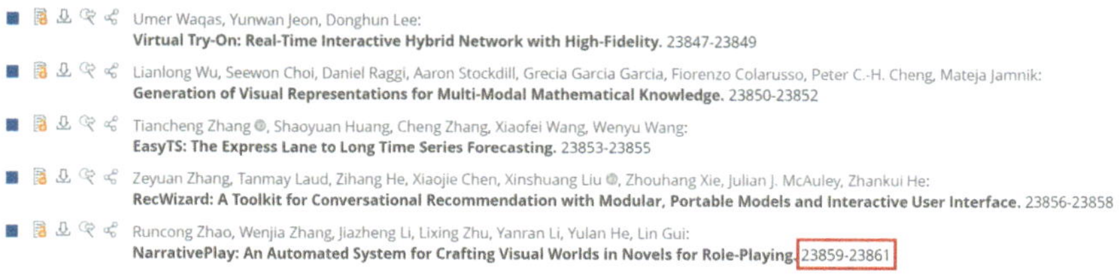
Umer Waqas, Yunwan Jeon, Donghun Lee:
Virtual Try-On: Real-Time Interactive Hybrid Network with High-Fidelity. 23847-23849

Lianlong Wu, Seewon Choi, Daniel Raggi, Aaron Stockdill, Grecia Garcia Garcia, Fiorenzo Colarusso, Peter C.-H. Cheng, Mateja Jamnik:
Generation of Visual Representations for Multi-Modal Mathematical Knowledge. 23850-23852

Tiancheng Zhang, Shaoyuan Huang, Cheng Zhang, Xiaofei Wang, Wenyu Wang:
EasyTS: The Express Lane to Long Time Series Forecasting. 23853-23855

Zeyuan Zhang, Tanmay Laud, Zihang He, Xiaojie Chen, Xinshuang Liu, Zhouhang Xie, Julian J. McAuley, Zhankui He:
RecWizard: A Toolkit for Conversational Recommendation with Modular, Portable Models and Interactive User Interface. 23856-23858

Runcong Zhao, Wenjia Zhang, Jiazheng Li, Lixing Zhu, Yanran Li, Yulan He, Lin Gui:
NarrativePlay: An Automated System for Crafting Visual Worlds in Novels for Role-Playing. 23859-23861

Fig. 4.4 The last five papers of the dblp records in the AAAI 2024 conference. (Obtained from https://dblp.org/db/conf/aaai/aaai2024.html)

We expect that the numbers of publications of all conferences/journals will continue to increase in the future since (1) more undergraduate students would like to undertake the postgraduate studies and (2) some subfields in computer science, e.g., artificial intelligence (AI), computer vision (CV), natural language processing (NLP), deep learning (DL), large language model (LLM), and data science (DS), start affecting other subjects (e.g., chemistry and physics (AI for science)), which can further arouse the interest from more students to join.

Furthermore, reading a paper line-by-line (and cover to cover) does not mean the reader can understand that paper. Some papers (especially for theoretical papers) involve a lot of details (e.g., cumbersome proofs), which can possibly distract the reader. Instead, the reader may understand more if they can summarize the paper in a high-level way[1] (but not include many details).

Therefore, instead of thoroughly reading a lot of (probably not important) papers, a student needs to understand which parts of each paper should be important for reading and which parts should be skipped. Here, we illustrate how to adopt the inverted triangle approach to filter those papers (see Fig. 4.5). Note that the student can already filter a lot of papers based on reading the titles. As an example, suppose that the student wants to conduct research related to spatiotemporal data management. He/she can skip those papers related to graph data management or relational data management. Once the student identifies some attractive papers based on the titles, he/she can directly read abstract/introduction of these papers during a short period of time (maybe a coffee break). With this short period of time, he/she can further identify some important papers. As an example, suppose that the student develops interest in working on kernel density visualization. He/she can skip those papers related to other types of visualization (e.g., scatter plot) after he/she reads the abstract/introduction. After the student has found that the title and abstract/introduction are interesting (and are worth for reading further), he/she can read the preliminaries and related work by identifying some missing research studies (e.g., there are other missing papers that are related to kernel density visualization). Only a few important papers (e.g., direct competitors) need to be thoroughly read by the student. Here, we further consider the first author of this book as an example. When he worked on the research paper

[1] This skill is very important for writing a survey paper and the related work section of a research paper.

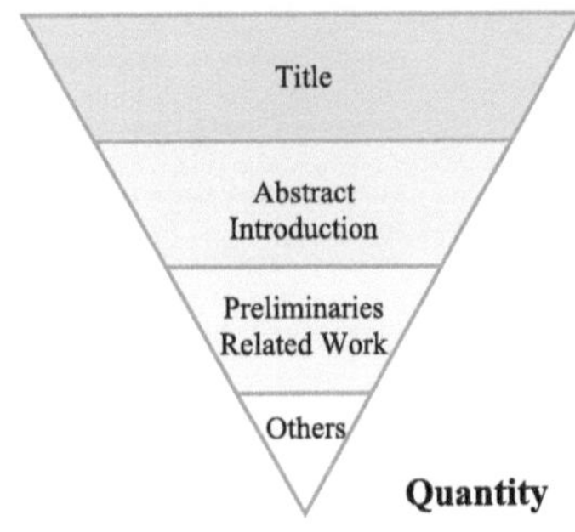

Fig. 4.5 The number of reading papers should follow this inverted triangle

"KARL: Fast Kernel Aggregation Queries", which has been published in ICDE 2019, he only read three papers thoroughly (and read many papers partially), which are the following three papers.

- Edward Gan and Peter Bailis. Scalable Kernel Density Classification via Threshold-Based Pruning. **SIGMOD 2017**.
- Alexander G. Gray and Andrew W. Moore. Nonparametric Density Estimation: Toward Computational Tractability. **SDM 2003**.
- Thomas Seidl and Hans-Peter Kriegel. Optimal multi-step k-nearest neighbor search. **SIGMOD 1998**.

Based on the above discussion, we can know why it is impossible and not wise for researchers to read every paper line-by-line (and cover to cover). **Remember that a very good and productive researcher only fully reads a few papers.**[2]

4.3 Ask Incorrect Questions

Many students (especially for junior students) may say that they are hard to find their own research problems although they have read many research papers and have asked a lot of questions regarding those papers. Some students may even mention that they struggle to find a research problem for nearly a year. However, after we investigate how they read research papers, we discover that most of these students may directly dig into the details without understanding the background of their research problems. Using Fig. 4.6 as an example, this student may want to find one research topic to work with. As such, he/she searches for the dblp record and (randomly) finds out one SIGMOD paper. However, he/she may skim-read or even skip the abstract and introduction and directly goes through the technical sections. It is very natural for many computer science students to do this because they may think that they are

---

[2] By reading this sentence, you need to be careful that it does not encourage you to avoid reading papers because of your laziness. You must not say this to your supervisor if you do not want to work.

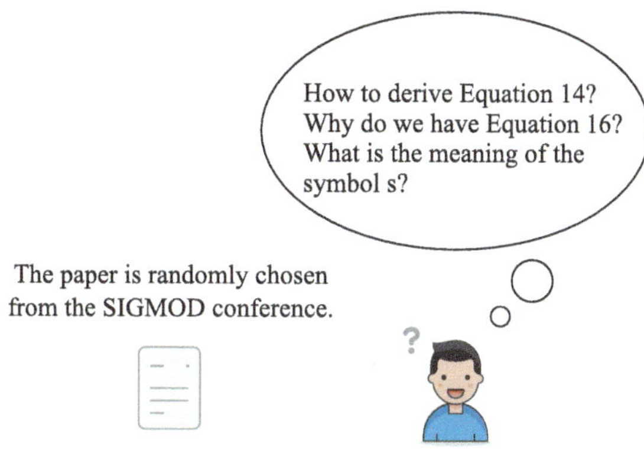

Fig. 4.6 Many junior students can ask incorrect questions for finding new research topics when they are reading papers

technical guys, who are good at developing algorithms but do not need to listen to a story. Therefore, they may ask a lot of questions about the details (e.g., "How to derive Eq. 14?" in Fig. 4.6). However, these questions are unlikely to help them find new research problems/directions. Instead, they should carefully read the abstract and introduction so that they can easily ask some questions that can open up a new direction. Using Fig. 4.1 as an example, when the authors have mentioned that they can improve the efficiency of generating a KDV-based hotspot map in abstract and introduction, the readers can ask some questions regarding the problem settings.

(1) Can we improve the efficiency of supporting the spatiotemporal hotspot map?

(2) Can we improve the efficiency of exploratory operations (e.g., zooming and panning) for the KDV tool?

As a practical example, we illustrate how the first author of this book found new research topics from September 2017 to April 2021 by asking correct questions in Fig. 4.7. Note that those references from [a] to [i] in the figure are shown as follows.

a **Tsz Nam Chan**, Man Lung Yiu, Leong Hou U. KARL: Fast Kernel Aggregation Queries. **ICDE 2019**.

b **Tsz Nam Chan**, Reynold Cheng, Man Lung Yiu. QUAD: Quadratic-Bound-Based Kernel Density Visualization. **SIGMOD 2020**.

c **Tsz Nam Chan**, Leong Hou U, Reynold Cheng, Man Lung Yiu, Shivansh Mittal. Efficient Algorithms for Kernel Aggregation Queries. **IEEE TKDE 2022**.

d **Tsz Nam Chan**, Zhe Li, Leong Hou U, Reynold Cheng. PLAME: Piecewise-Linear Approximate Measure for Additive Kernel SVM. **IEEE TKDE 2023**.

e **Tsz Nam Chan**, Pak Lon Ip, Leong Hou U, Weng Hou Tong, Shivansh Mittal, Ye Li, Reynold Cheng. KDV-Explorer: A Near Real-Time Kernel Density Visualization System for Spatial Analysis. **VLDB 2021** (Demo track).

f **Tsz Nam Chan**, Zhe Li, Leong Hou U, Jianliang Xu, Reynold Cheng. Fast Augmentation Algorithms for Network Kernel Density Visualization. **VLDB 2021**.

g **Tsz Nam Chan**, Pak Lon Ip, Leong Hou U, Byron Choi, Jianliang Xu. SWS: A Complexity-Optimized Solution for Spatial-Temporal Kernel Density Visualization. **VLDB 2022**.

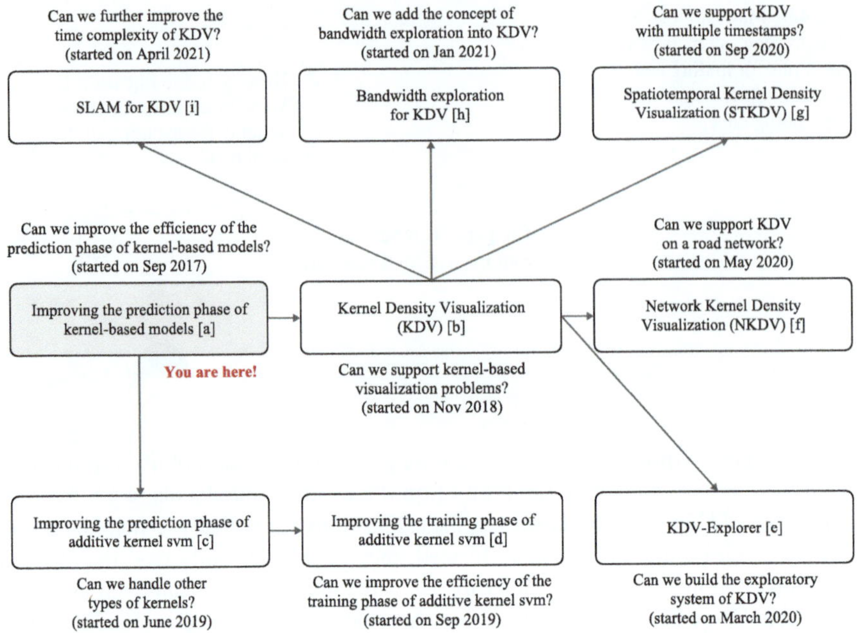

Fig. 4.7 This is how the first author of this book asks correct questions to discover new research directions from September 2017 to April 2021

h **Tsz Nam Chan**, Pak Lon Ip, Leong Hou U, Byron Choi, Jianliang Xu. SAFE: A Share-and-Aggregate Bandwidth Exploration Framework for Kernel Density Visualization. **VLDB 2022**.

i **Tsz Nam Chan**, Leong Hou U, Byron Choi, Jianliang Xu. SLAM: Efficient Sweep Line Algorithms for Kernel Density Visualization. **SIGMOD 2022**.

Based on the above discussion, we further emphasize that **only the above question type (related to problem settings) can significantly help students find new research directions**. Therefore, those students should frequently ask this question type (but not to ask for the details) when they are searching research problems.

4.4   Never Care Much About Writing Papers

Many students may think that conducting computer science research is to (1) learn state-of-the-art technology from research papers, (2) develop new algorithms/systems, and (3) writing code. They may think that writing a paper should be an easy task, which can be done in a few days, if all those new solutions/techniques are available. Therefore, they may imagine that all they need to do is to sit down, drink a coffee, and think of new solutions/techniques. When the supervisors ask them to write somethings, they may think that this is an interruption of their thoughts (just like interrupting Albert Einstein). Therefore, they may arbitrarily write somethings and return them to their supervisors. Ultimately, these students will find that they have zero (or nearly no) progress for their research papers and observe that their colleagues (with correct mindsets) have already submitted 5 to 6 papers to (and with one to two papers accepted in) top-tier venues in a year. At that time, some of these (especially for those cocky) students may think that the productive colleagues may just write some "water" papers (This word comes from Chinese, meaning that those papers are extremely incremental and not important), which cannot advance the state of the art. They will possibly keep this habit and think that they will ultimately have some big ideas that can change the world. But before these ideas come true, they may finally graduate with no paper (or with some weak papers) so that no university wants to hire them (i.e., leaving the academia forever). Even worse, some of them may be kicked off from research labs and never graduate with MPhil/Ph.D. degrees.

In addition, some students may think that their MPhil/Ph.D. supervisors will help them edit those research papers. Therefore, they will not treat those writing tasks (assigned by their supervisors) in a very serious way. They may think in this way. "My supervisor will help me revise the paper. Let me arbitrarily write it and send it to my supervisor." If my students really do this kind of things to me, I will blame them seriously. First, the supervisor needs to handle a lot of issues (e.g., writing proposals, writing books, writing research papers, writing patents, teaching courses, preparing teaching materials, attending conferences, attending MPhil/Ph.D. defenses, and having administrative meetings), which can possibly be ten times busier than those students. Second, the supervisor should have no responsibility for the MPhil/Ph.D. degree given that the student is lazy. Third, students can no longer learn the writing skills and earn the writing experience if they do not care much about those writing tasks.

Although learning new technology, developing algorithms/systems, and writing code should be the important components of conducting computer science research, **writing should be regarded as the most important component of conducting computer science research.** If students do not write, no one can know what they think (even they may have big ideas). Therefore, they must treat this to be the serious task during the MPhil/Ph.D. studies.

4.5 Avoid Writing Before the "Inspiration" Comes

Many students may say that they have no inspiration (a.k.a. no idea) for writing. They may also argue that they do not know what to write next. Because of the above issues, the last time for opening latex or overleaf can be several months ago (i.e., they do not edit papers for several months). One example can be found in Fig. 4.8 (in the overleaf). This is how we collaborate with another group of researchers. Note that the last time for updating this paper is four months ago and the first author only has this research task.

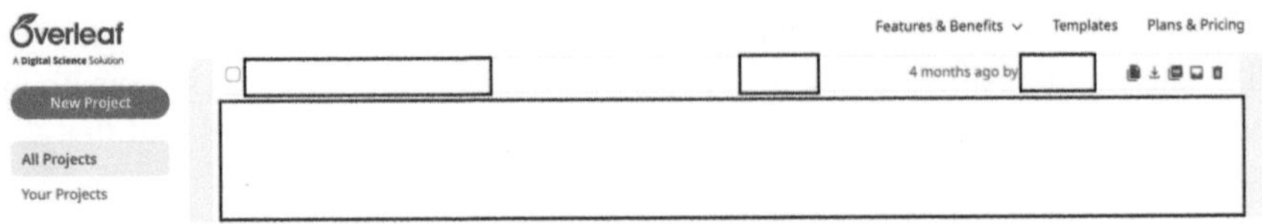

Fig. 4.8 There is no update for the paper in four months. Due to privacy issues, we hide some parts with white rectangular boxes

At first glance, it seems that their argument is correct. Suppose that students do not have any idea. What should they write? However, once you ask them about the progress regularly, they will always say somethings similar to you (e.g., They have no idea. The idea is not good. They are now thinking about the idea.). Then, we wonder why they do not have any idea for writing in a long period of time. Finally, we figure out some possible situations for those students.

Some students just sit down in a library/an office and start thinking about ideas. They think that those ideas will suddenly jump out if they sit for a long time. Suppose that you belong to this type of students. Then, we will ask you. Have you ever successfully established the complete solution in your brain? Here is our answer. We reckon that most of them find that their brains are still blank and nothing comes out even though they sit for a long time. Although some of these students can catch some small ideas during a few hours (very lucky), they may forget them after they have done other things (e.g., replying to emails, checking messages from WeChat/WhatsApp, browsing the Internet, chatting with their friends, and buying a cup of coffee). Several months later, they may discover the same idea again (i.e., they do not have any progress in these months and their brains get lost.).

After we discuss the above situations with those students, they totally agree with us and wonder why we know their situations so well. It is because a brain is normally in chaos and it is very easy to be distracted by other things. Using Fig. 4.9 as an example, everyone has a lot of stuffs in the brain. As an example, he/she may be worried about the relationship with the girlfriend/boyfriend. As another example, he/she may also get distracted by the melody of a new song. With a lot of stuffs in the brain, it is very hard to focus on thinking the research ideas. Even though you can discover the new ideas (and is satisfied with the progress for that day), it is easy to lose those ideas (with the reason that the brain is in chaos, which is hard to store complicated stuffs related to research ideas.).

Based on the above discussion, we can immediately know that it is very hard to establish a full solution to a research problem in a brain. Moreover, it is also very easy for a brain to forget the idea. Therefore, we cannot simply think, wait for the "inspiration" to come, and then write papers. Instead, we need to write in the very early stage. Note that writing is the creation process, which forces the writer to concentrate on what he/she writes. Therefore, it can help avoiding other stuffs (e.g., girlfriend and songs) to interrupt the writer, which can increase the chance for having inspiration (i.e., new idea). In addition, once the new idea is discovered, the writing

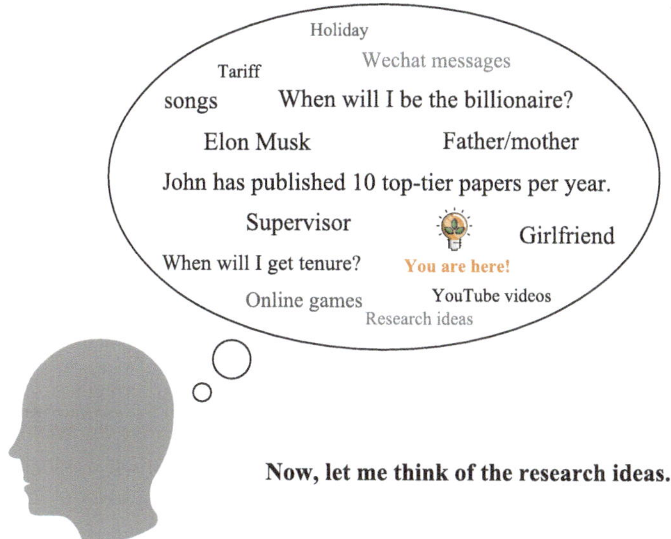

Fig. 4.9 The brain can be in chaos even though you want to think of the new research ideas

process can record this idea so that it will not be (re)discovered again and again. As such, **we can say that it is not "inspiration leads to writing". Instead, it should be "writing leads to inspiration".**

4.6 Avoid Writing Before the Idea is "Perfectly" Tested

Many students may say somethings like this.

(1) "I do not write the paper because I still need to conduct more experiments for testing my idea."
(2) "I need to compare my method with the additional baseline method. Therefore, I do not want to write the paper until I have seen the result." (Note that he/she has already compared the method with some existing methods and obtained the results.)
(3) "I need to thoroughly test my method in order to verify whether it can really advance the state of the art in order to determine whether it is worth for me to write this paper or not."

At the first glance, we may think that these students are very rigorous and are serious about the experiments. However, once we ask them about their progress in the next week (or month/or even year), they will reply you in the same way. Then, we immediately know that they may have either the following three issues.

(1) Excuses for not conducting research. Some students say this because they may only have a rough idea (or even no idea) for how to push the progress of their research. They may have no motivation for searching possible solutions. But they still need to pretend to be hard-working so that other people can admire them. For those students, we would like to say that this is the most childish thing. In reality (of research), only awards, publications, patents, monographs, research grants, and systems, etc., can be counted as research outcomes. No one cares about how they work hard toward conducting experiments, writing code, or testing ideas. Suppose that they would like to waste time for pretending to be "hard-working" students. They should consider whether they can (1) find a way to advance their research or (2) find somethings that are worth for them to do (maybe they can leave academia. Mark Elliot Zuckerberg (the co-founder of Facebook/Meta) also dropped out Harvard University.).

(2) Excuses for not writing papers. Indeed, some students are willing to conduct research. However, they do not have enough knowledge for (or do not like) writing papers. Therefore, they choose to write code/conduct experiments, which should be the relatively easy tasks, in the daily time. For those students, we would like to point out that the less papers they write, the less writing experience they can gain. We know that it is very painful to start writing an article, especially for the first one (the junior students). All of us have this kind of painful experience before since we did not have any knowledge of academic writing when we started the postgraduate studies. However, when you look back to your life, you will realize that you must have other types of painful experience for learning. As an example, when we learned the topic of Mathematical Induction in high school, it also took us a long time to be skillful for using this to prove whether the mathematical statement is correct (by doing a lot of exercises). You also got through it at that time. Therefore, why do you avoid writing academic papers? Note that the academic writing skills, which may be used for your next 30 to 40 years in your academic life, can be more important than Mathematical Induction.

(3) Easy to give up ideas. Some students say this because they really want to thoroughly (or perfectly) test the idea before writing. Note that every idea should have its weakness (i.e., no perfect idea). Otherwise, we can see that each textbook in the computer science field only discusses one (so called the best) solution. In addition, it is also not necessary to have so many researchers in many fields. Therefore, as shown in Fig. 4.10, if students do not write and figure out the weakness of the idea, they may be frustrated and think that they should give up this idea (or even move to the next topic). Why do they easily give up this idea? It is mainly because they have no draft. As such, the students (1) think that it has no cost to move to the next topic, (2) saving the idea is very tired, (3) focusing on the same topic is also very tired for them, and (4) changing to the new (fresh) topic is good. However, if students write regularly, they will have the draft with many pages (e.g., eight pages in Fig. 4.10). Once they figure out the bad performance for their idea, they have the high cost for giving up. What is the reason? Since they have already written many pages (e.g., eight pages), they only need to write a few pages, e.g., four pages (the number of pages for a lot of venues is 12.), in order to submit this paper to a venue. As such, it is not wise (or takes high cost) for them to give up this topic.

Fig. 4.10 Easy for students to give up ideas with no draft

Based on the above discussion, **we further emphasize that there is no perfect idea. In addition, aiming "perfect" might be the excuse for you not to conduct research/write papers. Keep writing every day.**

4.7 Never Write Regularly

Many TV shows describe that the top scientists have this kind of behaviors. First, they sit on a chair and wait for the inspiration (the big idea) comes. Second, they are always "brainstorming" (do everything in their brain). Third, they develop a big physical system that can change the world. Therefore, many new postgraduate students may be misled and think that conducting research is to (1) make themselves clever, (2) wait for their brains to provide novel ideas, and (3) only report when big experimental outcomes are available. However, none of these TV shows mentions that those scientists need to write papers regularly. Worse still, many recent news (especially in China) report that some students may have written a lot of incremental ("water") papers. Although we also do not encourage students to write these incremental research papers (which cannot benefit their careers), these news may easily be misinterpreted by those students (especially the junior ones) that writing papers are relatively not important.

In fact, writing regularly is a very important step for conducting research. For us, we believe that this should be the most important step (even more important than performing experiments). The main reason is that a draft is a concrete thing, which can show the current understanding of the writers. When you write, this draft can automatically tell you what you should do next (Of course, you need to keep asking questions.). As an example, when you get stuck for writing because you are not very familiar with some parts of related research studies, the draft will tell you to check those related studies. As another example, when you get stuck for writing because some experimental results are not available, the draft will tell you to conduct those experiments.

Many students may still wonder why they need to write papers regularly. They may argue that the brain should be responsible for thinking ideas. However, as we mentioned before (in Fig. 4.9), the brain is normally in chaos, which may contain a lot of stuffs. As such, even though the students may come up with great ideas, they can forget some critical details or even the whole ideas after they have performed other tasks, e.g., checking the WeChat message, gathering, and taking a rest (see Fig. 4.11). In contrast, the students can immediately further elaborate the ideas that they thought before once they have marked down those ideas in the draft (see Fig. 4.12).

Here, we further use this analogy for illustrating the importance of writing papers. We think that everyone plays role-playing (computer) games before. For each of these games, the main character needs to (1) go to different places, (2) fight with different monsters, and (3) fight with several bosses in order to win this game. Normally, it takes a long time for each player to finish the game. Therefore, each game allows the player to save a record so that the player can start from this record next time. I think

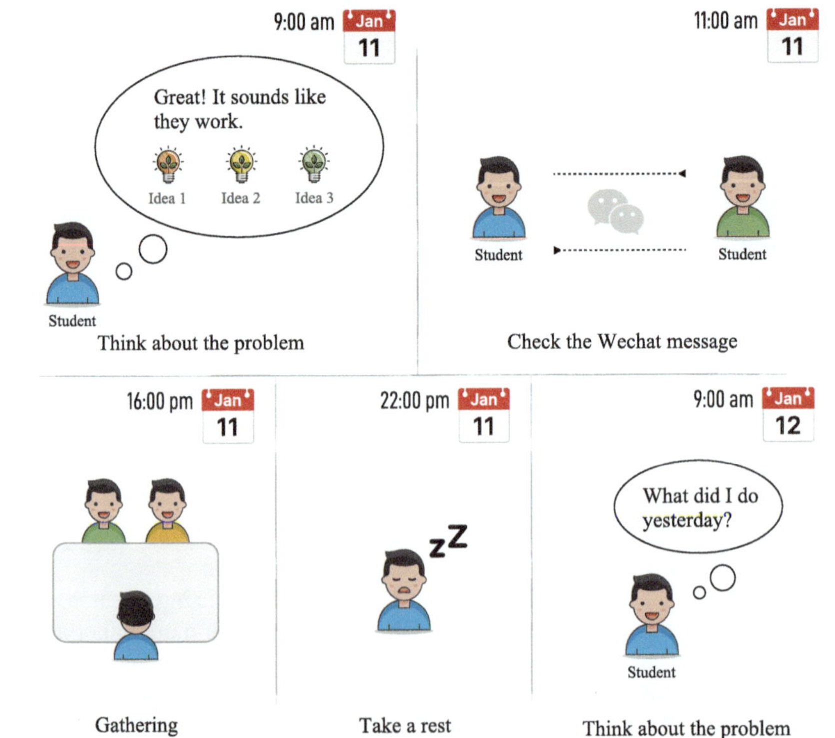

Fig. 4.11 Researchers who do not write are hard to have any progress in research

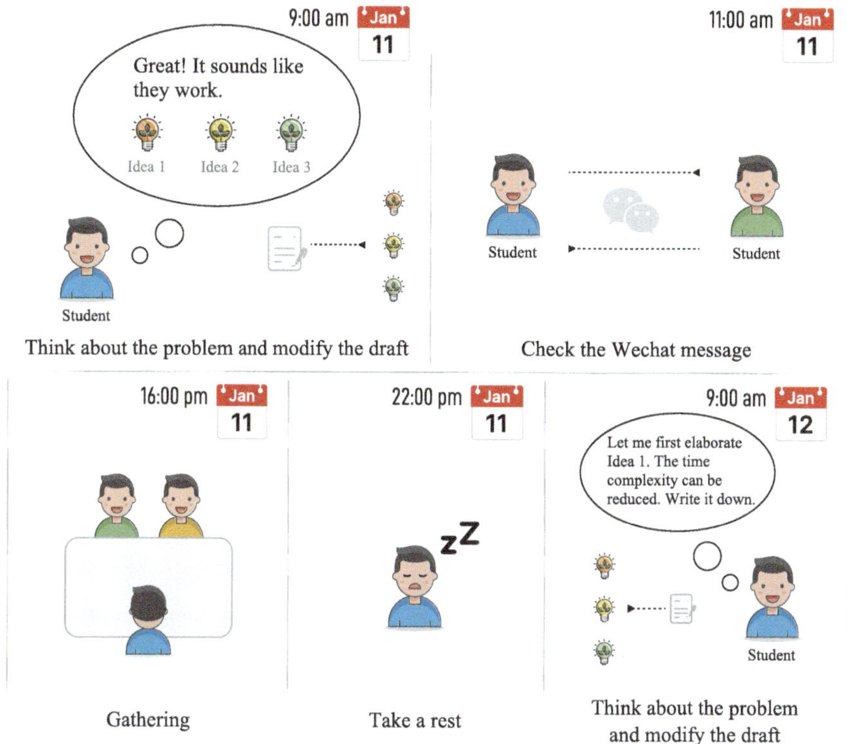

Fig. 4.12 Researchers who write regularly can normally have progress in research

everyone must save the record when he/she plays this game. Otherwise, they will start this game from scratch again. In fact, we can regard that writing a paper is the same as saving a record in a game. If we do not write, we need to start thinking ideas from scratch (see Fig. 4.11) as the brain may not be able to store the ideas (given that the brain has a lot of stuffs). If we write, we can start thinking on top of those ideas that have been recorded last time (see Fig. 4.12).

Based on the above discussion, we know that **writing regularly is the way to record what we have done in our research, which can significantly help the progress of our research.**

4.8 Avoid Writing Because of No Mood

Many students do not write research papers because they have no mood for writing. Indeed, this reason is very natural because academic writing is difficult. The brains from these students can easily turn to blank when they see the blank page of the

Ending: This student never has good mood for writing during the Ph.D. study and is kicked out from the research lab.

Ending: This student can only write one to two sentences in the first few weeks. Later, he/she starts to gain confidence for writing and can write more (one to two paragraphs) after one month. He/she graduates with four papers in top-tier venues.

Fig. 4.13 No mood should not be used as an excuse for not writing

PDF that is generated by latex. Note that we also had this experience before (even for now), especially for some papers that we do not know how to start writing them. At that time, some unproductive students may say that they have no mood for writing anything and then start doing other things, e.g., playing the online game (see Fig. 4.13). For those students, we would like to ask this question. When will you have good mood for writing? The answer is definitely never. The main reason for them to have no mood is the difficulty of writing papers. However, this type of difficulty exists forever, which indicates that these students will have no mood if they do not go through this type of difficulty.

One approach to go through this type of difficulty is to force themselves for writing one to two sentences every day (see Fig. 4.13). Initially, it can be very painful (hard to write even for one sentence). However, if the brain is getting used to it, that student does not feel very painful about this task and can start writing more (e.g., one to two paragraphs). Ultimately, that student may not say that he/she has no mood because he/she automatically opens the latex and writes somethings every day.

Using the first author of this book as an example. When he was in February 2016 to February 2017, he had worked on the following computer science topics (by reading several research papers).

- Template matching with deformable templates in pattern recognition (roughly February 2016 to March 2016)
- Route planning problems in road networks (roughly early March 2016)
- Locality-sensitive hashing (LSH) for similarity search (roughly March 2016 to April 2016)
- Document similarity search (roughly April 2016)
- Similarity search for non-metrics (roughly May 2016 to July 2016)

- Clustering (roughly July 2016 to August 2016)
- Manifold learning (roughly September 2016 to October 2016)
- Time series similarity search (roughly November 2016 to early January 2017).

However, he always felt no mood (or was not motivated) for writing any research paper. As such, he had not written even one page of a research paper at that period and changed research topics frequently. Once he felt that he would have the graduation issue and had read the slides[3] from Dimitris Papadias for stating that "a draft is something concrete–otherwise you may have done nothing as far as I am concerned.", he started to force himself to write several sentences when he started the new topic of Earth Mover's Distance similarity search in February 2017 (He sent the first incomplete draft (with 1.5 pages) to his supervisor on 8th February 2017). Initially, it was a painful process for him as he did not write a lot before 2017. However, after several months later, he started to see that the written draft automatically guided him what to write/do next. Therefore, he started to have a mood for opening latex to write several sentences every day. Ultimately, this paper was finished in September 2017 and submitted to VLDB 2018. Although this paper was rejected by this conference, this is the end for him to (1) have no mood for writing, (2) do not know what to do next, (3) have no progress in research, (4) change research topics frequently, and (5) have no research outcome. This paper was later also accepted in IEEE TKDE, which is a prestigious journal in data engineering.

- **Tsz Nam Chan**, Man Lung Yiu, Leong Hou U. The Power of Bounds: Answering Approximate Earth Mover's Distance with Parametric Bounds. **IEEE TKDE 2021**.

After he finished working on this paper, he then used nine months (from September 2017 to June 2018) for writing another paper, which was later accepted in ICDE 2019. After graduation, He started writing research papers in a rapid way and published a lot in SIGMOD, VLDB, ICDE, and TKDE (from 2019 to now) as a first author/corresponding author (especially when he was a research assistant professor in Hong Kong Baptist University and a distinguished professor in Shenzhen University). Now, he never says that he has no mood for writing because it is a habit for him to write every day.

4.9 Avoid Writing Because Their English is Not Good Enough for Writing

We believe that this is indeed a barrier for students (especially for those non-native speakers) not writing papers. Some students may not use English frequently and may have a very painful experience for learning this language in primary/high schools. In

---

[3] The link of the slides is https://home.cse.ust.hk/~dimitris/Instructions%20for%20PhD %20Students.pdf.

some countries, including China, Germany, France, South Korea, and Japan, most of those undergraduate students take computer science courses in their own native languages, who cannot have the chance to use English in class. Therefore, they fear for using English to communicate with others, let alone to write a 12-page English article (with double column) in a very rigorous way. Here, we would like to point out our thoughts regarding this issue.

You should be proud of using English. Some students may think that they will mainly reside in their own countries in the future. Therefore, they will raise this kind of questions. Why do they need to learn English? This kind of mindsets is in fact wrong. For us, mastering an important foreign language should be regarded as a glory, which can have a lot of benefits. Using China as an example, everyone can speak Chinese. If you also use Chinese there, no one will think that it is very surprising (see Fig. 4.14). But imagine that you can use fluent English to communicate with others (see Fig. 4.15). We would say that other people will definitely admire you. What is the reason? It is because they do not have this important skill but you have. Once you are proud of using English, you will definitely have the motivation to learn it. As such, this is the most important step toward learning English.

The best way to get rid of fearfulness for writing English is to write it. After the students are proud of using English, the next step is to get rid of the fearfulness of using this language. To achieve this goal, they need to force themselves to write a few paragraphs in English every day. For example, many students need to read papers every day. But most of them simply read those papers but do not write for what they have read. Summarizing papers in their own words (without any copy-and-paste from the original papers) is a great way for improving their English presentation skills. Moreover, many students may also conduct preliminary experiments. However, they do not write anything after they have conducted them. Note that summarizing experiments can also improve their English presentation skills. With more experiences, they can write the technical and introduction parts, which can further help them for

Fig. 4.14 It is not very special for someone (e.g., a Chinese person) to speak his/her native language (e.g., Chinese)

Fig. 4.15 Someone will admire you if you can speak an important foreign language (e.g., English)

gaining English presentation skills. Note that they need to read previous papers from top-tier venues in order to mimic the writing styles during the writing (learning) process. Although this process is very painful in the early stage, they will realize that this situation is getting better and better after a few months/a year (if they insist writing English every day). The main reason is that they get used to it.

Academic English is not that difficult compared with what you think. Some students may think that academic English must be very difficult. Indeed, when they are the newbies, it is very common for them to have this feeling. As an example, some specific terms/vocabularies in the papers may not be easily understood. As another example, their brains become blank (do not know how to start) when they try to write somethings in latex. However, after the students have read more papers, they will find that many similar sentence structures and vocabularies are reused again, which will automatically be stored in their brains. When the students practice more by writing some paragraphs regularly, they will realize that they can write these structures and vocabularies soon. In fact, writing a research paper in computer science does not need to have extremely solid English skills. There is no need for you to understand those books from Shakespeare or understand the law statements. To our understanding, we believe that the students with undergraduate degrees from computer science in many non-native English speaking countries (including China, Germany, France, South Korea, and Japan) also have enough English skills for reading/writing academic papers if they practice more.

The most difficult part for writing is not the language itself. Some students may argue that they cannot explain the concept clearly because they need to use English (the non-native language). However, once we ask them to explain the concept in Chinese (the native language), they still cannot be able to explain it clearly. The main reason is that they cannot understand the concept clearly or they have not learned the correct methodology for presenting the concept so that it is hard for audience to understand. Under this circumstance, what they need to do is not to blame for their "poor" English. Instead, they need to further understand this concept or learn for the presentation/organization skills. Nowadays, there are many software tools, including ChatGPT and DeepSeek, that can help for improving the language of writing. Therefore, other parts, e.g., the presentation flow, can be more important compared with the language itself.

Based on the above discussion, we need to encourage some students to be proud of using English. Moreover, we also want to highlight that academic English is not very difficult. By reading and writing more, they can ultimately get rid of fearfulness for using this language to publish research papers. Note that **practice makes perfect.**

4.10 Avoid Writing Because the Initial Draft Will be Ultimately Erased

Many students (especially for junior postgraduate students) may have this kind of experience before. He/she writes the draft and sends it to his/her supervisor. Then, the supervisor can have a lot of suggestions for the draft so that it needs to be significantly revised. More specifically, the student may have spent a week for writing 100 sentences and drawing two figures in an initial draft. In the next version, as suggested by the supervisor, 80 sentences and these two figures are significantly revised. Some of them may even be removed. Based on this experience, many students may think that this process is very painful since they have done a lot of "useless" work (i.e., "waste" a lot time). Some students may even think that they should not write even a single word until they have the "perfect" plan for writing (in order to avoid "useless" work). For those students who do not write any word, we will ask them one question. Have they ever thought of the perfect plan so that they can write the paper in one shot? If yes, how much time do they spend for writing one paper? For my opinion, I think most of them may have never successfully written a complete paper. Even though they have (luckily) completed one paper, they must have spent a lot of time (much more than the time for those students who write regularly).

In reality, it is very hard for everyone to know the next step if we do not try. Our brain cannot predict too many steps especially for the lack of information. Using the maze (see Fig. 4.16) as an analogy of writing papers, it is nearly impossible for the player to predict the correct route in the starting point of the maze. Therefore, the only way to win this game is to adopt the trial-and-error approach to walk through different routes. Although it can be painful for the player to choose the wrong routes (e.g., routes 1, 2, and 3 in Fig. 4.16 can reach the dead end.), these (wrong) routes can provide additional information (i.e., hints) for guiding you to choose the correct route (e.g., route 4 in Fig. 4.16). Therefore, only the players who try can be successful and earn additional experience (and can be confident for playing the next (probably more complicated) maze).

Note that writing a paper is similar to walking through a maze. Since the student may not be very familiar with the topic initially (i.e., does not have enough infor-

Fig. 4.16 The winner and loser for walking in a maze

mation) and does not have enough writing experience, it is very easy for him/her to make mistakes for writing a paper (i.e., walk to the dead end). However, during the interactive process with his/her supervisor, he/she can learn more (i.e., gain more information and experience) so that his/her draft will be improved. As an example in Fig. 4.17, the 1st version can be very bad, which can be full of mistakes and the solution is not well-designed. But we need to note that the following versions can be continuously improved. What we mean is that writing the "very bad" version is not a waste of time. Without this version, it cannot guide you to have the next (better) version, and thus is impossible to achieve the perfect version (i.e., the 6th version in Fig. 4.17). Note that writing a paper is also similar to eating bread. We are full because we have eaten six loaves of bread. But it is not because we eat the 6th loaf of bread.

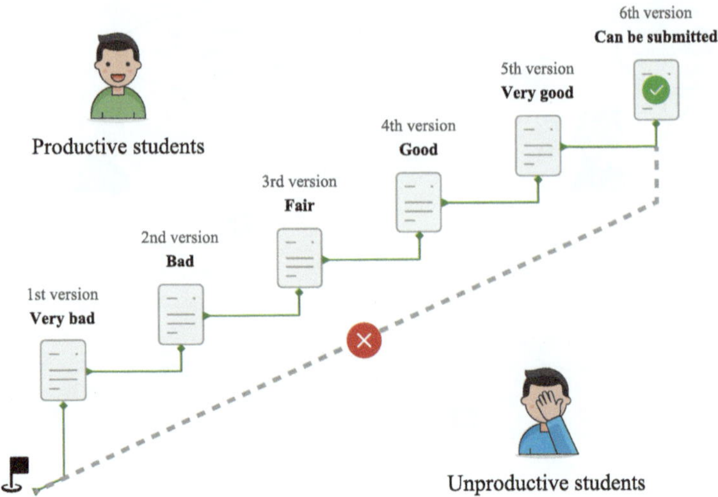

Fig. 4.17 Productive students write a lot of versions of their papers, while unproductive students simply "think" to achieve the perfect version

Given the above discussion, it is nearly impossible for a student to write a perfect paper in one shot. **A productive student writes a lot of versions of his/her paper, where each version is improved compared with the previous version, until that version is good enough for submitting to a top-tier venue.**

4.11   Avoid Writing Because of Busyness

Many students may say that they do not write because they are very busy with other things, e.g., coding, thinking ideas, working on assignments, having a tutorial class for students, and meeting with others. For those students, we would like to emphasize that this reason can possibly be an excuse for not writing papers (see Fig. 4.18).

The major goal for postgraduate students is to produce research outcomes. Many students may have a lot of activities every day. Some of these activities may not be related to research. Those students have many activities because they have a lot of free time during the postgraduate studies (Note that it is not mandatory for students to stay in offices during the working hours.). Therefore, it is easy for those students to have bad time management (or become lazy for research). For example, it is possible for students to be busy with playing online games and watching movies during the working hours (can even be from day to night). Although students can enjoy the free time (we regard it as a kind of academic freedom) during the postgraduate studies, they need to understand that they have the responsibility for producing research outcomes (research papers). Therefore, students are expected to assign a large portion

Fig. 4.18   The word "busy" can possibly be an excuse for not writing papers

of time for conducting research/writing research papers every day. They should not use the word "busy" as the excuse for doing somethings that are not research-related.

Students do not need to have a big block of time for writing. Some students may sometimes need to deal with a lot of trivial matters. Common examples include conducting tutorials for class, marking assignments, attending classes, meeting with others (e.g., supervisors and collaborators), and dealing with some matters from their families. Therefore, they mention that they only have the fragmented time so that they cannot work on anything. Some of them may even emphasize that the fragmented time is so little that they cannot turn themselves into the working mode. As such, they would argue that they can be productive when they have a big block of time (e.g., summer and winter holidays) for writing. However, when we dig into the details, we discover that those students still have at least one to two hours for the fragmented time every day, which are much more than enough for writing. Consider the first author of this book as an example. When he is a faculty member in Hong Kong Baptist University or Shenzhen University, he needs to (1) conduct lecturers, (2) prepare slides for classes, (3) attend meetings, (4) attend academic conferences, (5) give talks in different universities, (6) review papers from academic conferences and journals, (7) become the organizing committee members in some conferences, (8) make questions/answers for assignments/examination papers, (9) deal with teaching issues from students, (10) meet with his postgraduate students, (11) attending defenses from undergraduate/master/Ph.D. students, (12) handle the reimbursement and purchasing issues, and (13) deal with administrative issues from the university. Therefore, his daily time can be much fragmented compared with postgraduate students. However, he utilizes those fragmented time in a much better way. Note that he continues to push the paper/book/patent application even though the fragmented time is smaller than an hour (or even half an hour). As an example, he took a flight from Hangzhou back to Shenzhen on 30th November 2024. At that time, he waited for the plane (with 30-min fragmented time), he still managed to finish the patent application form there. As another example, he taught two courses, attended several defenses, and dealt with other issues in the spring semester of 2024/2025, he still managed to write this book during his fragmented time. Therefore, we reckon that there is no need to have a big block of time for writing. In fact, some other books, e.g., "How to Write a Lot: A Practical Guide to Productive Academic Writing" by Paul Silvia and "Writing Your Journal Article in Twelve Weeks" by Wendy Laura Belcher, also emphasize that it is not necessary for writers to have a big block of time to write in order to be productive.

"Coding" may be useless without writing. Some students may say that they cannot write because they are busy with writing code. For those students, we would like to ask this question. Do you find that coding can help you push the progress of your research work? If your answer is no, we would like to say that you simply write code without any goal. Consider the first author of this book as an example. He worked on one research topic related to improving the efficiency of solving the kNN search with non-metrics from May 2016 to July 2016. At that time, he wrote a lot of code for testing different methods. However, he only regarded writing code as the goal and did not know what to do next after he finished this task. For example, he did not provide any comprehensive analysis for results, did not ask further questions, and did not write research papers. Therefore, his code and his results are useless since they do not further push his research. Here, we emphasize that coding without writing can be useless (see Fig. 4.19). Instead, the best way for having progress in research is to let writing drive for other tasks (see Fig. 4.20), including coding.

4.12 Never Write Seriously Because my Supervisor Will Help me

Many students think that their supervisors will help them revise papers. Therefore, they are not very serious about their writing tasks, which are assigned by their supervisors (see Fig. 4.21).

Here, we emphasize that this mindset is completely wrong. Consider the first author of this book as an example. When he was a Ph.D. student, he conducted

Fig. 4.19 Coding without writing can be useless for pushing the research progress

research related to template matching from September 2014 to February 2016. At that time, he also had this kind of mindset (i.e., did not seriously write papers). Therefore, although his supervisor had helped him rewrite two papers, which were published in SSTD 2015 and TKDE 2017 (a top journal), he did not gain a lot of experience about how to write a research paper. Worse still, he did not learn how to ask research questions (and thus the problem finding skills). Therefore, he suffered a lot from February 2016 to February 2017 (see the example in Sect. 4.8). As another example, we have also heard from some students who published many decent papers during the MPhil studies cannot publish research papers when they are in the Ph.D. studies from another university. The main reason is that their MPhil supervisors are very nice for helping them rewrite the paper so that they are unable to learn the skills.

Based on the above discussion, we would like to point out that only those students who seriously write research papers (go through a lot of painful issues by themselves) can gain experience so that they can learn how to independently conduct research. Otherwise, they can only be under the umbrella of their supervisors. Once they leave their research groups, their productivity can sharply drop because they cannot get any help from their supervisors anymore. Note that another situation is that

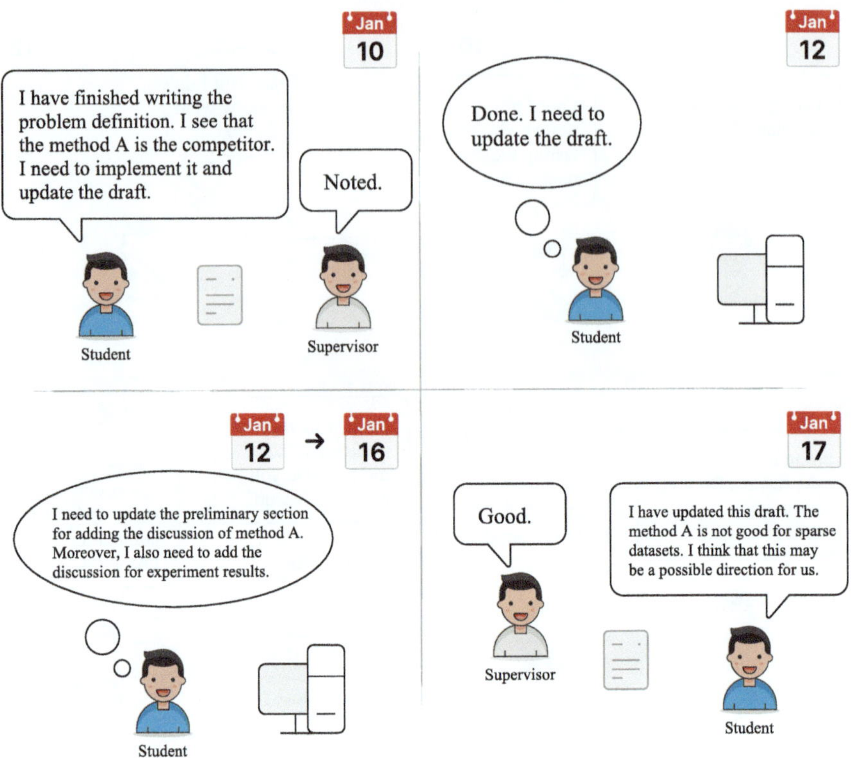

Fig. 4.20 Writing should be the best way to drive for other tasks (e.g., coding)

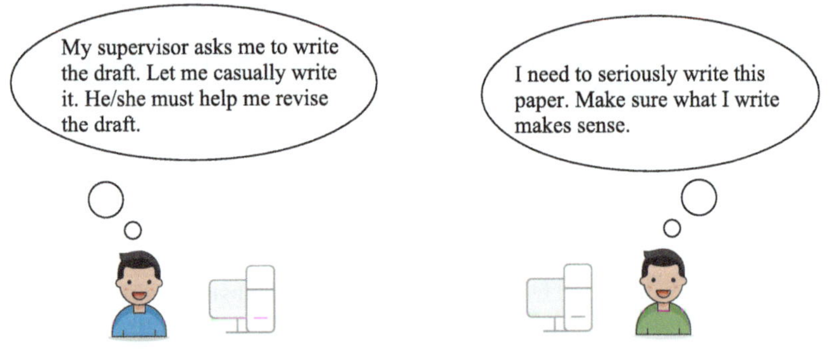

Ending 1: If the supervisor is nice, this student may get the paper accepted but cannot learn anything about writing.
Ending 2: If the supervisor is not nice, this student will be kicked out from the research lab.

Ending: May be assisted from his/her supervisor in the first few papers. Later, he/she can write the paper independently without the help from the supervisor.

Fig. 4.21 You can only gain the writing experience when you write seriously

some supervisors are not very nice (or very busy). If their students cannot write research papers by themselves, they will be kicked out from the research groups or cannot graduate from the universities on time until they finish enough paper submissions/publications.

4.13 Blame Others for Not Understanding Their Drafts/Presentations

When students send their drafts to their supervisors, those responsible supervisors will read them and provide comments/additional questions to the students. However, some students may not be very happy about the thoroughly edited drafts (e.g., see a big cross for a paragraph and see many questions in the blank space) because they think that they have spent a lot of time for writing the drafts. Some of them may think that the supervisors are so stupid (see Fig. 4.22), who cannot understand (1) the "beauty" hidden in the draft and (2) how genius they are. These students may even question the ability of their supervisors (e.g., think that the supervisor cannot help them become the next "Albert Einstein").

For the above cocky students, they normally have no publication or very weak publications (e.g., papers in third-tier venues) because of the following reasons. First, these students still do not realize that this is the fault of the authors (not readers) if the readers cannot understand their papers. Second, the supervisors guide them for writing well-structured papers. However, the students refuse to learn it, indicating that these students cannot improve their presentation ability to the level of top-tier venues. Therefore, when they want to judge the ability of their supervisors, we would like to say this to them. "Go to the personal homepage of your supervisors and check how many top-tier publications they have before you judge their ability. Then, go to your personal homepage and see how weak you are."

Fig. 4.22 Unproductive students normally blame supervisors for the poor presentation of their papers

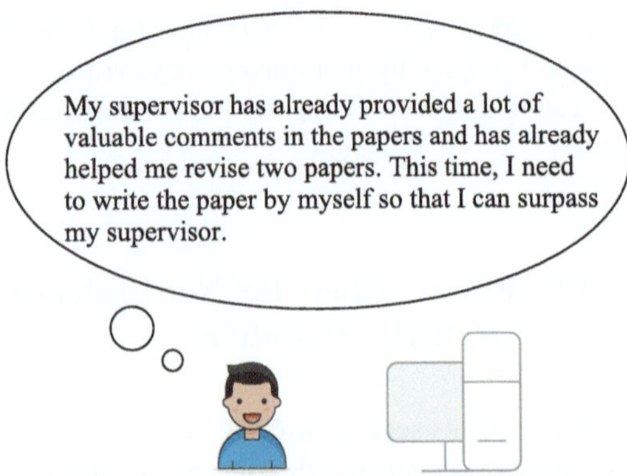

Fig. 4.23 Productive students normally follow the suggestions (especially for those presentation-related suggestions) from their supervisors and improve their drafts so that they can ultimately surpass their supervisors

Compared with the above unproductive (and cocky) students, some productive students are happy to accept comments from their supervisors so that they can learn from the comments for revising their papers. They will even take a look for those old papers from their supervisors in order to learn the writing style. With the training for a few years, they will discover that their abilities (including presentation skills and topic-finding skills) become closer to the ones of their supervisors. With more practices (by writing more papers), they will find that their supervisors spend less time for assisting them, indicating that they are stronger. Ultimately, these productive students will find that they can surpass their supervisors (see Fig. 4.23), who can conduct independent research.

4.14   Think That It Is Cool to Confuse Reviewers

Many students (especially for junior students) do not understand research papers after they read them. As such, they may then develop this mindset (see Fig. 4.24).

"Research papers must be written in a difficult way (e.g., full of complicated equations and complicated figures) so that other readers think that the authors have deep understanding about their research topics."

This mindset is indeed wrong. Writing a paper is similar to having a formal conversation between different researchers. If other researchers do not understand what you are talking about, this conversation is useless. Therefore, other researchers must not feel impressive about those "knowledge" that they do not understand. Maybe you can think in this way. If your friends, who also work in computer science research, say that they have developed a great algorithm but they cannot explain how great it is, you will not also think that this algorithm is great. Instead, you will have serious doubts about it. This situation is also the same when reviewers review your papers.

Ending: Graduation with no publication in top-tier venues.

Fig. 4.24 Illusion from students for writing complicated papers to confuse reviewers

If reviewers cannot understand many parts in your papers, they will also raise a lot of doubts about it. Obviously, with many doubts, they will ultimately give a "Reject" for that paper. Note that not many reviewers will give an "Accept" for a paper with a lot of doubts (especially for top-tier venues) because this is a responsibility for authors to present a paper so that readers can understand it easily. As a remark, for all research papers that (1) are submitted to top-tier venues, (2) are difficult to be understood, and (3) are reviewed by us, nearly all of them are rejected. We believe that other reviewers also have similar records.

Therefore, some smart students will be more considerate to the reviewers (see Fig. 4.25). They will assume that those reviewers do not have solid background for their research. Therefore, they will (1) draw some illustrative figures for explaining the core concepts (or ideas) and (2) make the paper more self-contained so that reviewers can easily understand how their techniques can advance the state of the art. Once reviewers are happy with the paper, it can significantly increase the chance for that paper to be accepted in a top-tier venue. Note that many papers (without any

Ending: Graduation with 5 publications in top-tier venues. Get a tenure-track assistant professor job in a prestigious university.

Fig. 4.25 A smart student simplifies the difficulties of the complicated paper in order to let reviewers easily understand it

fancy technique) can also be accepted in top-tier venues. The main reason is that they are well-written (e.g., the story is interesting and the technique sounds correct, which can work in practice compared with existing techniques).

4.15 Overcomplicate Somethings

Many students may tend to overcomplicate somethings when they are writing research papers and discussing with others, e.g., supervisors (see Fig. 4.26). They have this kind of mindset mainly due to the following three reasons.

Show that they are "knowledgeable"/"smart". Some students may think that discussing somethings in a complicated way can demonstrate that they are knowledgeable in their research topics or demonstrate that they are smart. We believe that they have this mindset because of some TV shows/movies, which depict that a "smart" scientist only talks about somethings that everyone (or at least a large portion of people) cannot understand. Therefore, they also need to follow this in order to be "smart". To be honest, we think this is the most childish mindset. First, a researcher

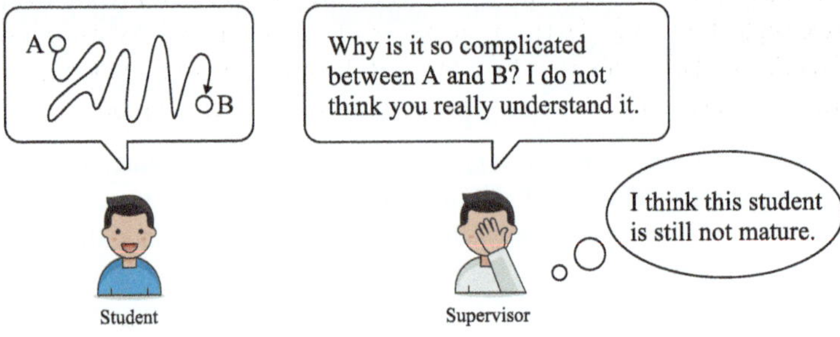

Ending: The discussion lasts for three hours.

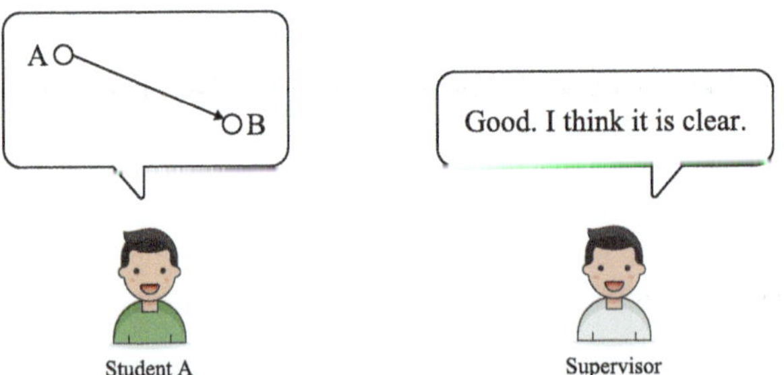

Ending: The discussion lasts for five minutes.

Fig. 4.26 Never overcomplicate somethings. Otherwise, it is a waste of time for both you and your supervisor

is knowledgeable in one research area because he/she has already provided solid contribution to it (e.g., publish a lot of top-tier papers or establish a great system that has been used by a lot of users) but it is not because he/she has made a lot of overcomplicated (a.k.a. useless) discussions for it. Second, a smart researcher only presents a complicated concept in an easy/intuitive way so that everyone in the same community (or even layman) can easily grasp the knowledge. This is very important because it can significantly reduce the communication time between different researchers.

Do not have enough technical contribution. Some students may discover that the technical contribution may not be enough. Therefore, they may try to add some unnecessary content (e.g., equations) into some sections in order to make the paper look "high class" (see Fig. 4.27). They may think that this is the only way to get rid of the comment of "not enough technical contribution" from the reviewer. However, we would like to point out that it is not very difficult for reviewers to determine the necessity of technical content (especially for those reviewers with solid reviewing experience) although reviewers may not be familiar with the research topics of the

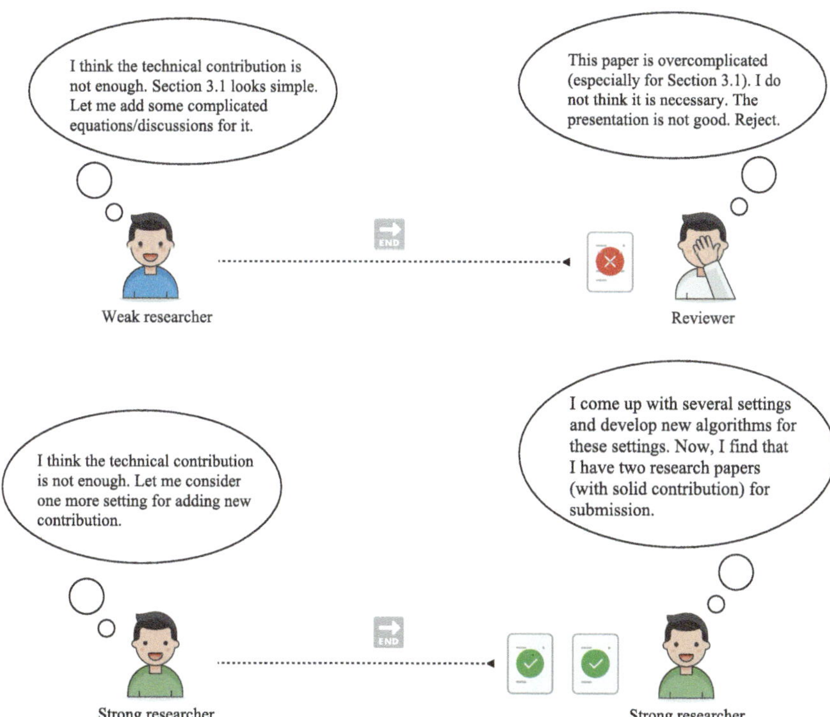

Fig. 4.27 Weak researchers can overcomplicate somethings for their poor technical contribution, while strong researchers use the correct approach (i.e., think of new contributions/problem settings) for addressing this issue

authors. Using the first author of this book as an example, he has reviewed one paper that has been submitted to a VLDB conference recently. He discovered that the paper has developed four algorithms for solving one problem. However, the first three algorithms are overcomplicated and not necessary. Therefore, he raised one question to the authors for asking why they need to make these unnecessary methods and also expressed the concern for the technical novelty/contribution of that paper. Ultimately, that paper has been rejected by the conference. Hence, the correct approach for solving the issue of "not enough contribution" is to think of new contribution or add new problem settings (see Fig. 4.27). There is no other approach to get rid of it.

Do not understand the concept well. If some students do not understand the concept well, it is normal for them to discuss it in a very difficult way. However, some students may still insist that they understand the concept very well even though they state that they cannot express it in an intuitive/easy way. Here, we need to emphasize that the concept must be easily explained by a student if he/she can understand it well enough (see Fig. 4.28). If it is still very complicated for the student to explain it, we

Fig. 4.28 If you have understood the concept, you must be able to express it in an easy way. Otherwise, you do not understand it well enough

can ensure that this student must not be able to understand this concept well enough. Therefore, what the student needs to do is to (1) take a look for that concept again and (2) figure out how to express it to others. **Only those concepts that can be easily (and logically) expressed by the student should be regarded as understanding by that student.**

Chapter 5
Common Mistakes and Correct Mindsets for Presenting Research Papers

In this chapter, we discuss some common mistakes for presenting research papers that have been made by new postgraduate students (including us in the early stage of career), which have been categorized into the following thirteen types.

5.1 Never Write as a Reader

Many students may write papers only based on their own views, which means that they may assume that readers can understand what they are writing/thinking (see Fig. 5.1). However, we need to emphasize that readers are not smart and know everything, especially for the fast developing field like computer science. As an example, everyone talked about IoT/blockchain from 2019 to 2020, computational epidemiology from 2020 to 2022 (in the COVID-19 period), LLM from 2023 to now, and AI for science from 2024 to now. Therefore, it is impossible for every reader to master the knowledge from a short period of time. Instead, many researchers can only stay in their own fields. Using the first author of this book as an example, he is dedicated to developing efficient algorithms for GIS operations and he knows nothing in other fields. Moreover, even for GIS, he cannot know everything, i.e., he only understands some specific parts, e.g., kernel density visualization and K-function, in GIS. Under this circumstance, students should assume that readers only understand minimal knowledge (e.g., assume that they just get the bachelor degree in computer science). When students write each paragraph (or even one sentence) of research papers, they need to keep asking whether readers can understand what they are writing (see Fig. 5.1).

Normally, there are several reasons for why readers cannot understand a paper, which are summarized as follows.

T. N. Chan and D. Wu, *Mastering the Academic Writing Mindset*,
https://doi.org/10.1007/978-981-95-4850-7_5

Fig. 5.1 Instead of simply writing what you think, you need to write a paper using the view from a reader

The motivation is unclear. Some (junior) students write a research paper for solving a research problem without having any motivation for why they need to solve it. Consider the following example.

"Kernel Density Visualization (KDV) [1] has many applications, including crime hotspot detection [2], traffic accident hotspot detection [3], and disease outbreak detection [4]. However, this operation is very slow. Therefore, we need to propose efficient methods for solving this problem."

After the student writes this paragraph for the introduction, he/she does not know what he/she should write next and sends it back to the supervisor. Then, the supervisor can ask many questions. First, what is Kernel Density Visualization (KDV)? The student should not assume that everyone knows the concept of KDV. Instead, he/she should clearly adopt an intuitive way to illustrate this concept (by drawing a figure like Fig. 4.1). Second, who are users? The student should clearly state this since readers may not understand who are using this tool. Third, how can KDV handle crime hotspot detection, traffic accident hotspot detection, and disease outbreak detection tasks? The student should clearly mention how these tasks can be handled by KDV using some words that can be easily understood by layman (instead of simply listing all these tasks). Fourth, is it necessary to support KDV? The student should realize that other tools (e.g., histogram) can also be used as hotspot analysis. He/she should motivate the importance of solving KDV. For example, many software packages also need to handle KDV. Fifth, how slow is the operation? Readers can have no concept for how slow KDV is. Therefore, the student should provide further evidences and the quantitative values so that readers can understand why it is important to solve this problem. By asking the above questions regarding the motivation. We can edit this paragraph in this way.

"Kernel Density Visualization (KDV) [1] has been extensively used in different domains, including criminology, transportation science, and epideminology. Criminologists and transportation scientists [2, 3] adopt KDV to discover crime and traffic/traffic accident hotspots in different regions. Epideminologists [4] adopt KDV to detect disease outbreaks in various geographical regions. Figure 5.2 shows how KDV can be utilized to generate a hotspot map using the Los Angeles crime dataset (i.e., those yellow points). Observe that the hotspot region is colored by red, which indicates that this is the dangerous zone. Since many domain experts have adopted KDV for performing visual analysis, many software packages, e.g., QGIS [5], ArcGIS [6], Scikit-learn [7], Scipy [8], and Seaborn [9], have already supported this tool.

However, KDV is a computationally expensive operation, which takes $O(XYn)$ time, where $X \times Y$ and n denote the resolution size and the number of data points (see those yellow points in Fig. 5.2a), respectively. Consider this Los Angeles crime dataset (with 1.26 million data points) as an example. Generating a 1280×960-resolution KDV takes 1.548 trillion operations. Therefore, KDV does not scale to support large datasets and high-resolution sizes. To address the efficiency issue of KDV, we need to develop efficient algorithms."

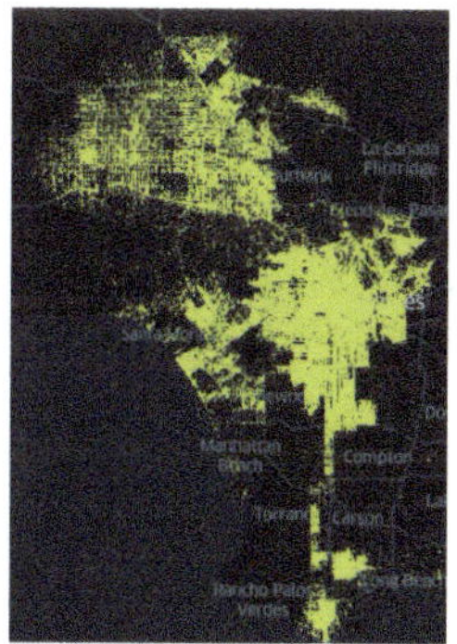

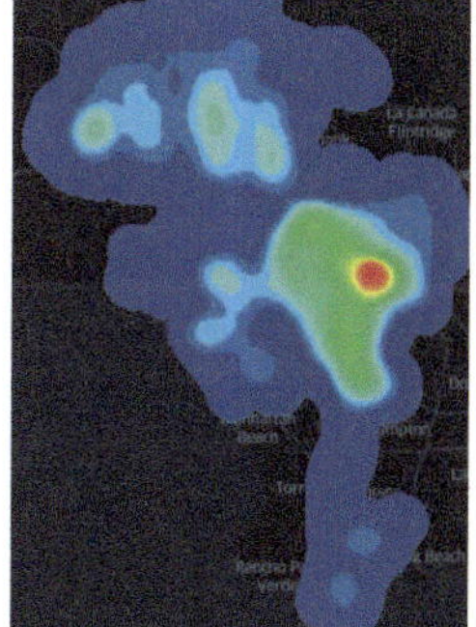

(a) Crime events in Los Angeles   (b) Hotspot map

Fig. 5.2 A hotspot map (based on KDV) for crime events in Los Angeles, where the red region is a hotspot. (Obtained from Fig. 1 in "Tsz Nam Chan, Pak Lon Ip, Bojian Zhu, Leong Hou U, Dingming Wu, Jianliang Xu, Christian S. Jensen. Large-scale Spatiotemporal Kernel Density Visualization. ICDE 2025")

By comparing these two versions, we note that the second version should be much more clear for readers to understand why we need to solve this problem. Students need to keep asking the above question types so that they can write papers with clear motivation.

The connection between paragraphs is broken. Some junior students may write some paragraphs that are not connected with each other. They may discuss A in the first paragraph and then discuss B in the second paragraph. However, A and B may not be straightly related and these two paragraphs do not have any connection in between. Here, we consider the following example.

"Kernel Density Visualization (KDV) [1] has been extensively used in different domains, including criminology, transportation science, and epideminology. Criminologists and transportation scientists [2, 3] adopt KDV to discover crime and traffic/traffic accident hotspots in different regions. Epideminologists [4] adopt KDV to detect disease outbreaks in various geographical regions.

In this paper, we would like to improve the efficiency of KDV by proposing the method XXX, which can significantly improve the efficiency by XXX compared with the existing methods."

In the first paragraph above, it discusses the applications and the users of KDV. However, in the second paragraph, it suddenly changes to discuss the new method that can improve the efficiency over the existing methods. Therefore, we can note that there is no connection in between (i.e., we cannot understand why the first paragraph can link to the second paragraph). Here, we need to emphasize that this mistake is very common for junior students (i.e., inexperienced writers), including us when we were young, because their brains can easily be in chaos (or blank) when they write the first few papers. Here, we would like to suggest that students can get several blank papers and draw the map for connecting somethings that they want to discuss. With this linkage (see Fig. 5.3), it can help students write papers in a more logically way.

Directly discuss the details without providing intuitive illustration. When some students write their new solution in one section, they simply discuss the details step-by-step. As an example, suppose that the student develops one algorithm with 20 lines, he/she simply discusses each line of the algorithm, which is similar to the following context.

"In line 1, our method scans all those data points and augment some additional terms on them. The time complexity of this line is $O(n)$. In line 2 to line 5, ..."

Here, we need to point out that a research paper is not a manual of a machine. Readers can feel extremely bored and can skip all these details (and of course do not understand) when they read somethings like the above context. Therefore, the authors should intuitively explain the concepts. Consider our recent (top-tier) research paper "Yue Zhong, **Tsz Nam Chan**, Leong Hou U, **Dingming Wu**, Wei Tu, Ruisheng Wang, Joshua Zhexue Huang. A Fast and Accurate Block Compression Solution for Spatiotemporal Kernel Density Visualization. **SIGKDD 2025**." as an example. In this paper, we need to propose the block compression method for reducing the dataset size so that it can improve the efficiency for computing approximate spatiotemporal

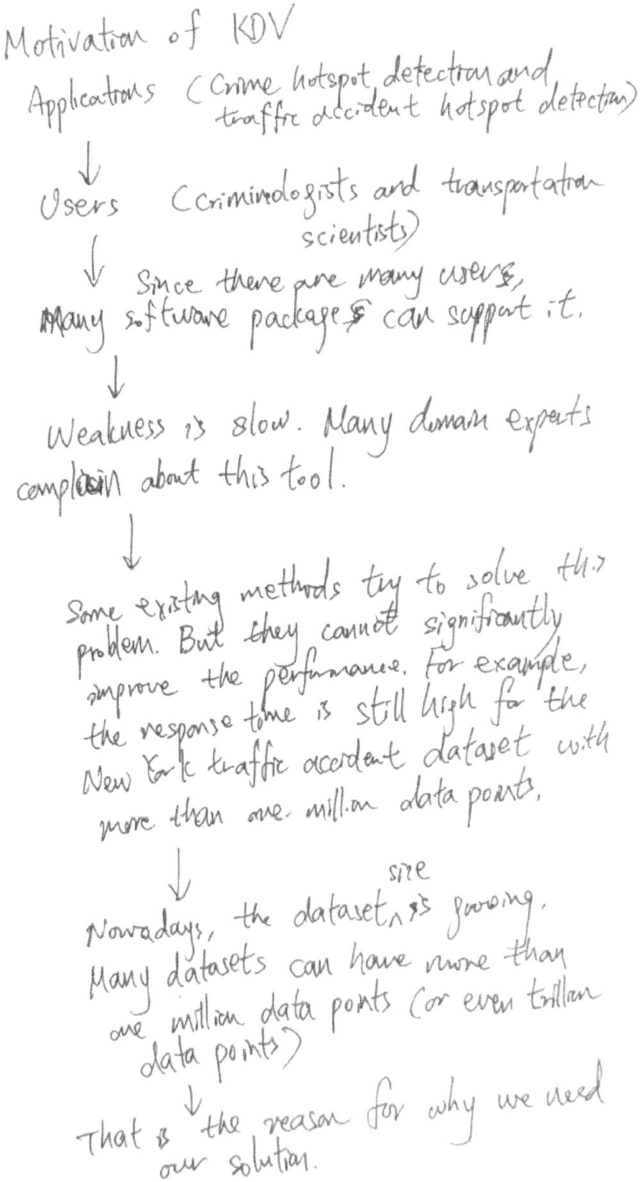

Motivation of KDV

Applications (Crime hotspot detection and traffic accident hotspot detection)

↓

Users   (criminologists and transportation scientists)

↓   Since there are many users,
Many software packages can support it.

↓

Weakness is slow. Many domain experts complain about this tool.

↓

Some existing methods try to solve this problem. But they cannot significantly improve the performance. For example, the response time is still high for the New York traffic accident dataset with more than one million data points.

↓

Nowadays, the dataset size is growing. Many datasets can have more than one million data points (or even trillion data points)

↓

That is the reason for why we need our solution.

Fig. 5.3 This is how the first author of this book draws the map in a paper to illustrate why we need to propose another efficient solution for solving the KDV problem

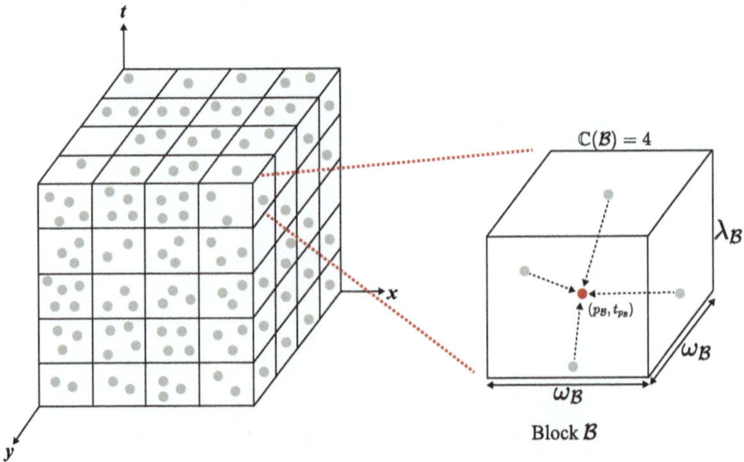

Figure 6: Illustration of the core idea of block compression, where each grey sphere denotes the location data point (p, t_p), the red sphere denotes the center point $(p_\mathcal{B}, t_{p_\mathcal{B}})$ of the block $\mathcal{B}$ (with size $\omega_\mathcal{B} \times \omega_\mathcal{B} \times \lambda_\mathcal{B}$), and $\mathcal{B}$ covers four location data points (i.e., $\mathbb{C}(\mathcal{B}) = 4$).

Fig. 5.4 The SIGKDD 2025 paper utilizes this figure to illustrate the concept of block compression. (Modified from Fig. 6 in "Yue Zhong, Tsz Nam Chan, Leong Hou U, Dingming Wu, Wei Tu, Ruisheng Wang, Joshua Zhexue Huang. A Fast and Accurate Block Compression Solution for Spatiotemporal Kernel Density Visualization. SIGKDD 2025")

kernel density visualization, i.e., STKDV (a variant of KDV). Although we also have the algorithm (see Algorithm 1 in that paper), we provide Fig. 5.4 to explain the concept. With the caption and the figure, readers can easily understand how the block compression method works without knowing the details of the algorithm.

The paper is not self-contained. A proposed solution can possibly depend on some concepts from existing research papers. Therefore, students may assume that reviewers should have the responsibility (or obligation) to understand those papers in the literature. Otherwise, these reviewers should not have the right to review their papers (see Fig. 5.5). However, this mindset is completely wrong. As pointed out in Fig. 2.12, the knowledge space of a reviewer is very small. For example, we always review papers (more than 99% of papers) that are not from our research areas. Therefore, it is not realistic to assume that reviewers can understand those concepts from existing research papers. Instead, an author should make sure that his/her paper is self-contained, which means the dependency should be clearly explained in the paper. Using the above **SIGKDD 2025** research paper as an example, that paper proposes the block compression solution (see Fig. 5.4), which can be combined with the state-of-the-art STKDV algorithms, SWS (published in VLDB 2022) and PREFIX (published in ICDE 2025). At that time, when we wrote this paper, we did not assume that readers have the knowledge about these two papers and provided intuitive examples to illustrate the core ideas of these two methods. Therefore, reviewers think that our

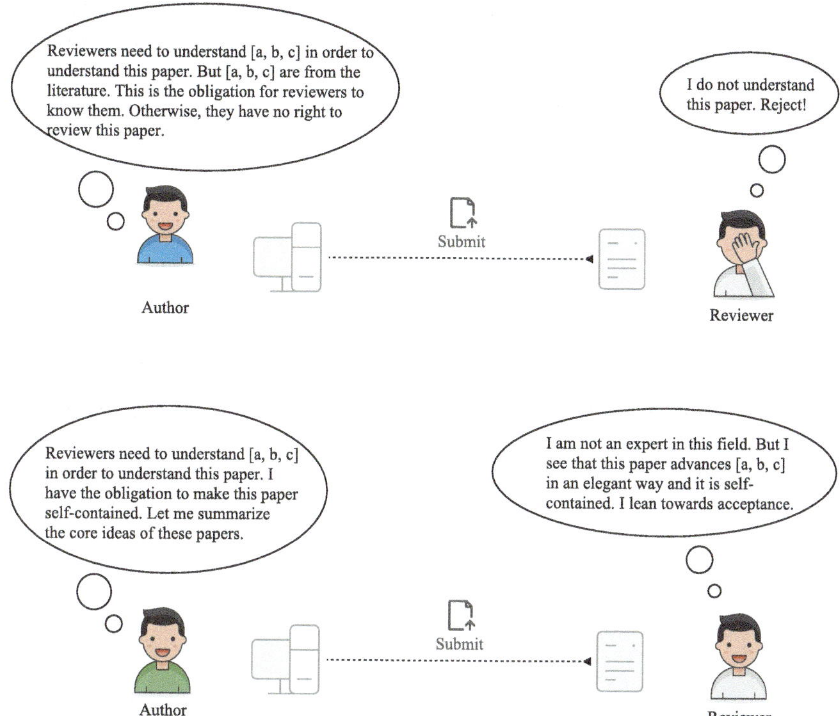

Fig. 5.5 An author must have the obligation to make a paper self-contained so that reviewers can easily understand it

paper is well-written and can understand how our paper advances the state-of-the-art solutions (PREFIX and SWS) even though reviewers may be not very familiar with our research paper (the confidence scores are 1, 1, 1, 2, and 2, which range from 1 (the lowest confidence) to 5 (the highest confidence)). Hence, we need to emphasize that this is the responsibility (or obligation) for a student to make a paper self-contained in order to let reviewers accept his/her paper (even though these reviewers may not be familiar with the research topic).

5.2 Never Tell a Good Story

Many (junior) students may think that computer science researchers only need to develop solutions for solving computational problems and telling a story should not be a job for them. Some of them may even think that telling a story is a kind of not engaging on honest work. Instead, they should develop a good solution so that it can "speak" for itself (or it can "win" compared with other solutions). Here, we need to emphasize that this mindset is wrong. Note that the goal of publishing a research paper is not to demonstrate that the authors are smart (or smarter than others). Instead, the goal is to show that they have solved some important and practical problems, which are raised from the society, by doing somethings (e.g., developing a new algorithm or building a new system) that can advance the state of the art for benefiting users. Therefore, there must be a story behind each research paper and this story can be much more important than the proposed techniques (because the story can ensure whether a research problem is worth studying or not). In other words, if a student can be able to tell a good story (like Fig. 5.6), it should be easy for this student to discover many future research problems (and thus, publish many research papers).

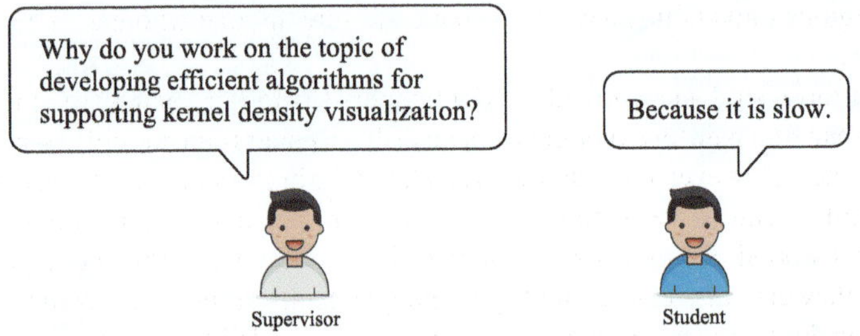

Ending: This student cannot publish a lot of papers because he/she cannot tell a good story for motivating a research problem.

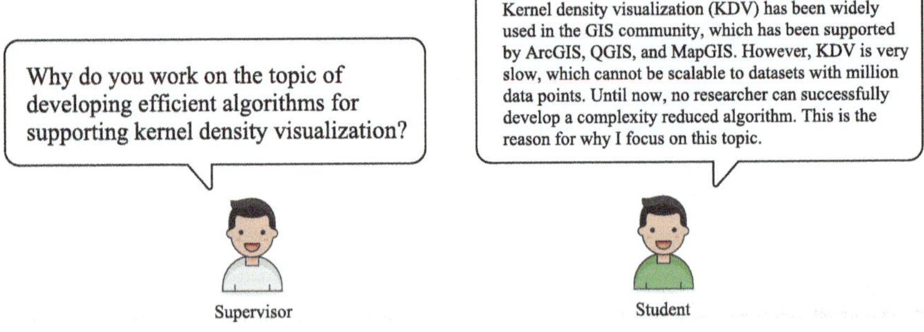

Ending: This student can publish a lot of papers by telling a lot of good stories to motivate a research problem.

Fig. 5.6 A productive student must be able to tell a good story for motivating a research problem

5.3 Never Act as a Salesman for Writing Papers

Many (junior) students may think that writing papers should be a serious issue. Therefore, they think that they should not provide any exaggerated claims and fake/falsified results in research papers. Here, we need to emphasize that we totally agree with this. Note that providing fake/falsified results (this is an ethical issue.) can even be the end of the career of students. However, those students should not have the wrong mindset that they cannot sell a research paper. In fact, selling a research work is an important skill for students. Consider selling apples as an example (see Fig. 5.7). We know that not every apple can be beautiful. Therefore, it is easy for a salesman to sell some apples that are not perfect. A bad salesman only reports the weakness of the apple (i.e., rotten). However, a good salesman can figure out some good things for his/her apple (e.g., pesticide-free, which means that the apple should be healthy).

Based on the above analogy, students need to realize that not every solution is perfect (i.e., every solution is likely to have its weakness.). For example, some solutions may suffer from relatively large space consumption, while other solutions may suffer from relatively high response time. However, reviewers (or buyers) only accept those papers (or buy somethings) that clearly show their advantages. Therefore, the student of a research paper should act as a good salesman for selling their research ideas by highlighting the goodness and mitigating the weakness (see Fig. 5.8).

Fig. 5.7 Selling apples (bad salesman vs. good salesman)

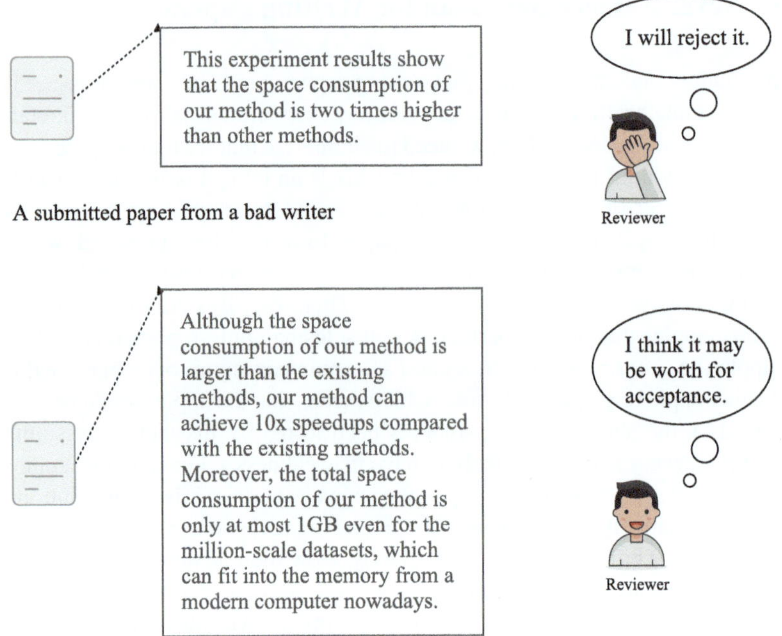

A submitted paper from a bad writer

A submitted paper from a good writer

Fig. 5.8 An academic writer is similar to a salesman

5.4   Write a Solution Before Having a Clear Problem

Some (junior) students may focus on writing (or thinking of) the solution. For example, they may want to develop a fast indexing method (e.g., a new tree structure) or a new machine learning model for improving the efficiency or the accuracy. However, when we ask them what research problems they are solving. They cannot answer us in a crystal clear way (see Fig. 5.9). For those students, we would like to emphasize that **we need to have a research problem first before we can have a solution for this problem**. It is impossible to reverse the order because there is no reason (or no motivation) to develop this solution. Therefore, students must clearly write down the problem statement (or the formal problem definition) first before they write the methodology part. Otherwise, the methodology part should be deemed as useless.

Note that some students may have the mindset that a solution should be more important than a problem. The main reason from these students is that a solution can be very "fancy", e.g., full of mathematical proofs, mathematical derivations, and complicated algorithms, which can somehow show their "intelligence". Unfortunately, we would like to point out that this mindset is completely wrong. A new research problem can be even more important than a new solution. As a reviewer in top-tier conferences/journals of computer science, we would like to point out that

Fig. 5.9 Some students conduct research for finding a new solution but they are still unclear about the research problem

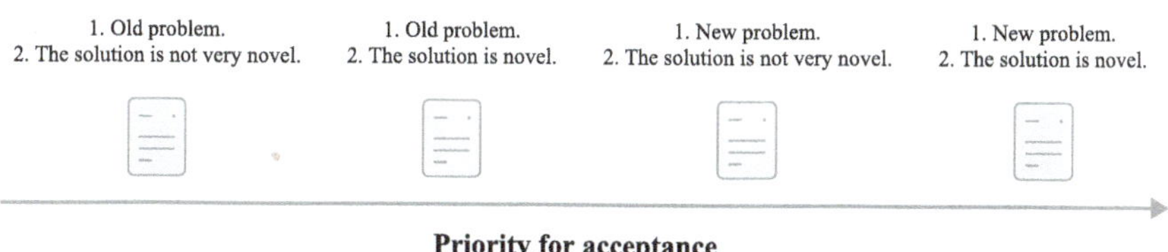

Fig. 5.10 A research problem can be more important compared with a solution

a new research problem can be regarded as a new research direction, which can possibly let many researchers focus on it in the future. To our understanding (see Fig. 5.10), reviewers normally have a higher priority to accept those research papers with new research problems compared with new solutions (especially for conference papers). Here, we further consider the first author of this book as an example. He had written two papers, which are (1) "LARGE: A Length-Aggregation-based Grid Structure for Line Density Visualization" and (2) "Large-scale Spatiotemporal Kernel Density Visualization". The technique in the paper (1) is mainly some lower and upper bound functions with the grid structure, which are not very novel (since many database researchers also consider using these two techniques before). However, since the research problem of "line density visualization" is the first time to appear in the database community, this paper is very successful to be accepted in VLDB 2025 without any rejection. In contrast, the paper (2) has solid technical contribution, which proposes a new data structure that can theoretically reduce the time complexity of generating an exact spatiotemporal kernel density visualization without theoretically increasing the space complexity. However, since the research problem of "spatiotemporal kernel density visualization" is not new, this paper is deemed to be not novel by reviewers and has been rejected five times before the acceptance in ICDE 2025. Therefore, based on the above discussion, we strongly suggest that students should think of a novel research problem.

5.5 Never Actively Draw Figures

Many students (especially for junior students) may not actively draw figures when they write research papers. Normally, they draw figures only after their supervisors tell them to do so. The main reasons are that (1) drawing a beautiful figure can take a long time compared with typing some words for explaining the concept and (2) they may not have enough experience for drawing figures. With these reasons, they avoid drawing figures in a paper. However, drawing figures is indeed the most important step for writing a good paper based on the following two reasons.

Fig. 5.11 This figure (copied from the New York Times news) is very intuitive, which shows a lot of information without writing even a single word

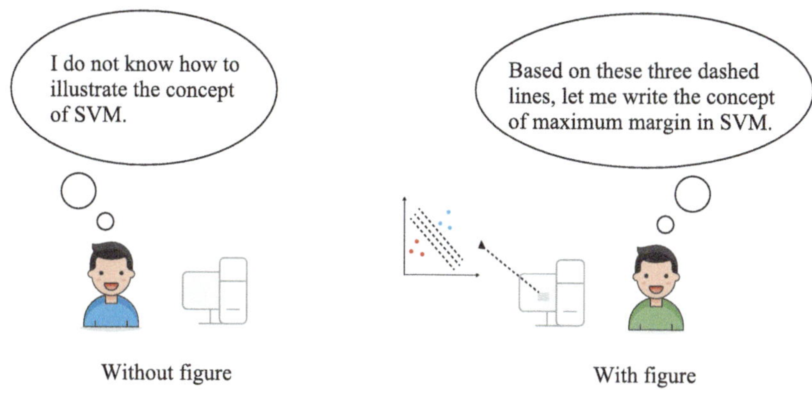

Fig. 5.12 Writing the concepts about SVM by students (with and without a figure)

A figure is worth a thousand words.[1] Figure 5.11 shows a G7 meeting in 2017 regarding political/economic issues between different countries. By solely looking at this figure (without writing even a single word), we can immediately obtain a lot of information. As an example, we can know that Angela Merkel (the chancellor in Germany at that time) must have a serious conflict with Donald Trump (the president in the US at that time) during the meeting. As another example, we can also know that this meeting should not be very successful. Since human can easily absorb information from images compared with information from text (i.e., figures are more intuitive compared with text), students should actively draw figures in order to make other people easily understand their papers.

A figure can easily guide a student to write words. When a student wants to explain a complicated concept without drawing a figure, he/she can discover that it is very difficult to write even a single sentence. The main reason is that some concepts are hard to be explained solely by text. However, once he/she has drawn a figure, he/she only needs to write words by referring to that figure, which can make his/her life much easier. Consider Support Vector Machine (SVM), which is a commonly used machine learning model, as an example (see Fig. 5.12). The student can easily explain the concept of maximum margin based on three linear lines (see black dashed lines) in the figure. However, without this figure, SVM is very difficult to be explained in an intuitive way.

---

[1] This figure can be found in the link https://www.nytimes.com/2018/06/10/world/trump-merkel-photo-g7-summit.html.

5.6   Never Seriously Draw Figures

Many (junior) students may not seriously draw figures when they are writing papers. Some of them may think that they are just computer science researchers but not artists. Therefore, they will ask these questions. Why do they need to seriously draw figures? Why not just arbitrarily draw figures? Here, we would like to emphasize that figures can be regarded as the soul of each paper. The main reason is that figures are very intuitive. As such, most of the readers can thoroughly read all figures in the paper. Therefore, if those figures are not seriously drawn, readers (or reviewers) cannot grasp a lot of useful information from that paper and can even have bad impression for authors (given that the figures are really bad). Here, we would like to point out some common mistakes that are made by students.

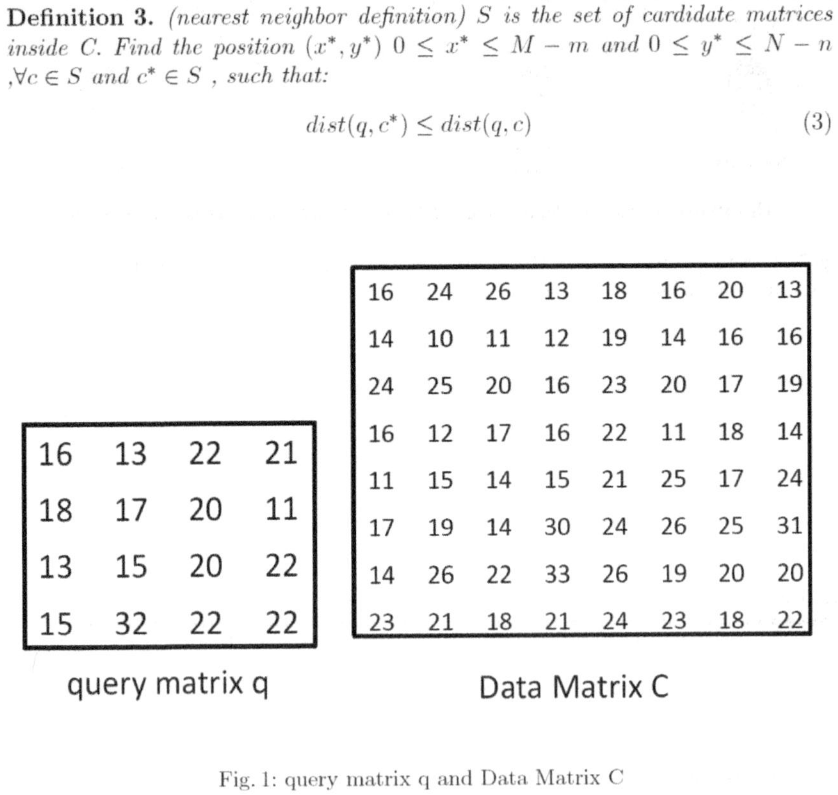

Definition 3. *(nearest neighbor definition) S is the set of cardidate matrices inside C. Find the position (x^*, y^*) $0 \leq x^* \leq M - m$ and $0 \leq y^* \leq N - n$,$\forall c \in S$ and $c^* \in S$, such that:*

$$dist(q, c^*) \leq dist(q, c) \tag{3}$$

query matrix q

16	13	22	21
18	17	20	11
13	15	20	22
15	32	22	22

Data Matrix C

16	24	26	13	18	16	20	13
14	10	11	12	19	14	16	16
24	25	20	16	23	20	17	19
16	12	17	16	22	11	18	14
11	15	14	15	21	25	17	24
17	19	14	30	24	26	25	31
14	26	22	33	26	19	20	20
23	21	18	21	24	23	18	22

Fig. 1: query matrix q and Data Matrix C

Fig. 5.13 Figure 1 was drawn by the first author of this book when he wrote the first paper in SSTD 2015. He was seriously blamed by his supervisor at that time

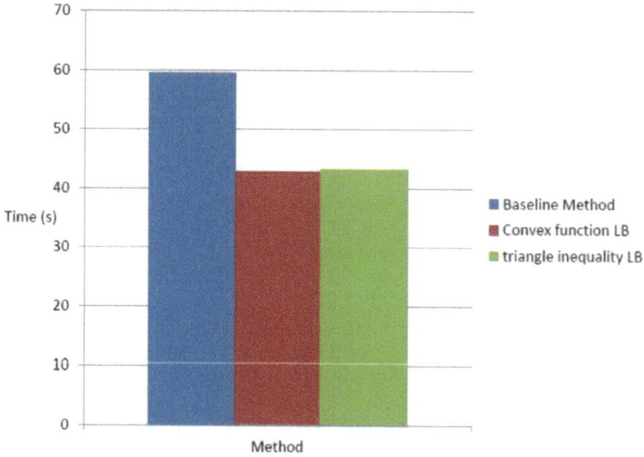

Fig. 11: scan and refinement efficiency result, p=2

6. Roger M. Dufour, Eric L. Miller and Nikolas P. Galatsanos, *Template Matching Based Object Recognition With Unknown Geometric Parameters* IEEE Transaction on Image Processing, vol. 11, no. 12, pp. 1385-1396, Dec. 2002
7. Y. Moshe and H. Hel-Or, *Video Block Motion Estimation Based on Gray-Code Kernels* IEEE Transaction on Image Processing, vol. 18, no. 10, pp. 2243-2254, Oct. 2009
8. Q. Wang and S. You *Real-Time Image Matching Based on Multiple View Kernel Projection* IEEE CVPR 2007
9. W. T. Freeman, T. R. Jones and E. C. Pasztor, *Example-Based Super-Resolution* IEEE Computer Graphics and Applications, vol.22, no.2, pp. 56-65, Mar/Apr. 2002

Fig. 5.14 Figure 11 was drawn by the first author of this book when he wrote the first paper in SSTD 2015. He was seriously blamed by his supervisor at that time

Do not accurately control the font size of the words in a figure. After a (junior) student draws a figure and put it into the PDF, he/she may not care about the font size of words, which can be either too big or too small, in a figure. In the view point of reviewers, they can think that this can make the paper look very strange (or not professional). Using Fig. 5.13 as an example, the font size of those numerical values in the "query matrix q" is too big compared with the font size of the text in the main content. Using Fig. 5.14 as another example, reviewers cannot read this figure clearly since the font size of the labels of the x-axis, the y-axis, and the name of each method is very small. Hence, a rule of thumb for drawing the figure is that the font size of words in a figure should be similar or slightly smaller than the font size of text in a paper.

Do not convey enough information. Consider Fig. 5.13 as an example. Figure 1 originally aims to illustrate the template matching problem. However, readers can

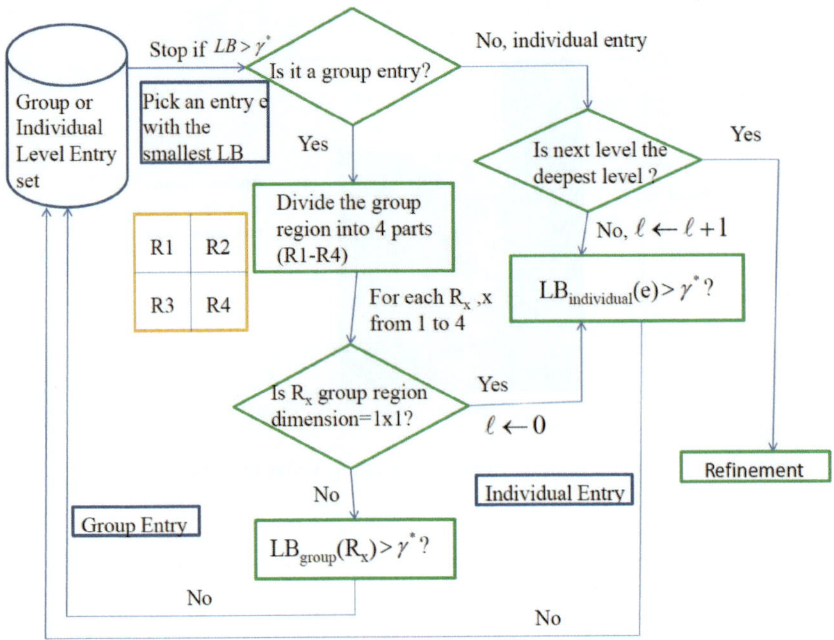

Fig. 6: The flow chart of our program

Fig. 5.15 Figure 6 was drawn by the first author of this book when he wrote the first paper in SSTD 2015. He was seriously blamed by his supervisor at that time

only see these two big matrices and cannot understand this problem by reading this figure (i.e., only obtain a small amount of information). Therefore, this figure is not useful and must be redrawn.

Put too many details in a figure. Consider the first author of this book as an example. His supervisor asked him to draw some figures to illustrate his algorithm. To respond to this question, he drew Fig. 6 in Fig. 5.15. However, this figure is very complicated, which contains many details, including mathematical inequalities, different branches, and complex terms (e.g., group entry, individual entry, and refinement). Based on this reason, readers cannot understand this figure in a short period of time. However, a figure is supposed to be easily understood, i.e., everyone can know what it conveys immediately. Therefore, if a figure cannot achieve this goal, that is not a successful figure, which must be redrawn.

Draw unprofessionally. To be honest, this is very hard to define. But it can be easily identified by many professional (experienced) writers. Using Fig. 5.15 as an example, this figure is very unprofessional. First, some arrows point to other components with different angles. A natural figure should not have these angles (can be either vertical or horizontal lines). Second, some words (e.g., "e" and "smallest LB" in "Pick an entry e with the smallest LB") stick to the boundary of the box. Third, the first letter of each word in "Group Entry" and "Individual Entry" is capitalized while other components are not. Students are encouraged to (1) learn how to draw professional figures by reading research papers in top-tier conferences/journals and (2) practice more by drawing more figures. By gaining more experience, they will notice that they can ultimately draw some professional figures.

5.7 Never Carefully Choose Notations

Many students may not carefully choose notations when they are writing research papers. Note that carelessly chosen notations can significantly affect the readability of a research paper, which can be easily detected by reviewers. Using the first author of this book as an example, he has already rejected various research papers in the past based on messy notations (leading to the difficulty of understanding those research papers.). There are several types of mistakes for those notations, which can be categorized as follows.

Use a long English word to represent a notation. Some students may not think deeply about the notation for representing each term. Instead, they may simply use the name of that term to be the notation. Using the formula of computing the speed of an object as an example, they can write this formula as follows.

$$\text{speed} = \frac{\text{distance}}{\text{time}}$$

Worse still, some terms may have multiple words. As an example, suppose that they want to find the density of objects inside a region A. They can write the equation in this way.

$$\text{density (A)} = \frac{\text{Num\_of\_Obj (A)}}{\text{Area (A)}}$$

Once we see these equations/notations, we can immediately have the bad impression for those authors. The main reason is that these symbols are not professional and those students do not seriously spend some time (probably at most one to two hours) to address this obvious issue. In a recent TKDE submission that was reviewed by the first author of this book, he has decided to reject that paper after he saw these unprofessional symbols (of course, that paper also suffers from other issues.).

Use different notations for the same term. Some students can be in chaos (may be the first few times for them to write research papers) when they are writing research papers. They can forget the notation that has been defined by them for a term before. Due to this reason, they can use another notation, which is close to the meaning of that term, when they write the paper. As an example, when they want to use the notation for the term "temporal distance (a.k.a. time range/temporal threshold)", it is possible for them to use these notations, which are t, d, r, and τ, "interchangeably". Therefore, many unnecessary notations can be easily identified by readers, which can lead to bad impression (e.g., readers can think that these students are careless and did not proofread the paper). To ensure the consistency, these students should frequently check those notations that have been defined by them before when they need to write equations or proofs.

Reuse the same notation for different terms. When some students write research papers, they do not care about which notations they have already defined before. Once they have encountered the discussion for one term, they directly define a notation that is closest to that term. As an example, when they need to use the notations for representing these two terms, time and temporal distance, they can simply choose the notation t to represent both of them. This can easily happen especially when there are many notations in a paper (e.g., theoretical paper). Note that readers can misunderstand the paper when the same notation refers to different meanings. In order to avoid this issue, once students need to define the notation of one term, we suggest that they should (1) stop for a while, (2) check the notations that was defined in a paper, and (3) decide the suitable notation for that term. With this approach, students can likely avoid reusing the same notation for different terms in a paper.

5.8 Never Care About the Consistency Issues for Writing Papers

Many students do not care about the consistency issues for writing papers. However, consistency issues of a research paper can be easily detected by reviewers in conferences/journals. Once these issues are detected, reviewers (including us) can have bad impression for that paper because these consistency issues can be easily addressed or avoided before submission. Here, we list two common consistency issues for writing computer science papers.

Use different names for the same term. When some students write different sections (maybe even for different paragraphs of the same section) in a paper, they can possibly use different names for the same term. Using graph data management as an example, both "node" and "vertex" have the same meaning. Worse still, some terms can have many names. For example, "template matching", "pattern matching", "nearest neighbor search on matrix", and "subwindow search" refer to the same term in the image processing and pattern recognition communities. Therefore, suppose that students use all these names interchangeably in the same paper, reviewers can notice that this paper is in chaos, especially for those reviewers who are not working on the same area, so that they can find reasons to reject it. Based on the above discussion, those students need to make sure that they use the same name for the same term throughout the same paper (see Fig. 5.16).

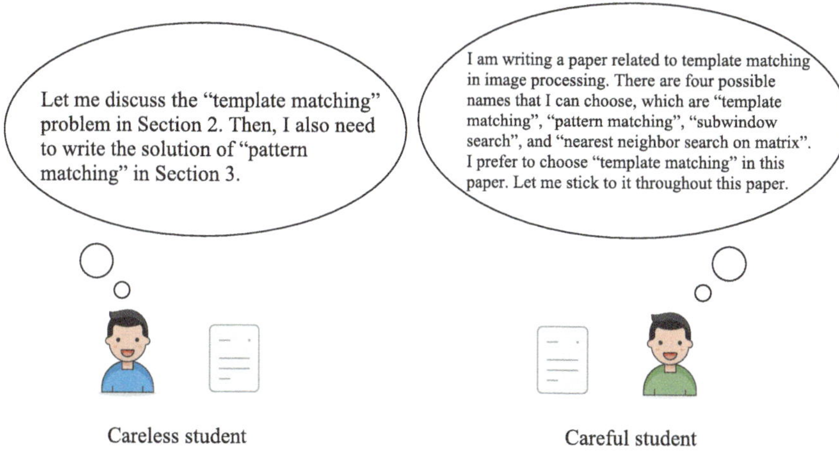

Fig. 5.16 A careful student makes sure that he/she uses the same name for the same term throughout the same paper, while a careless student does not care about it

The section titles are not consistent. Some students may not make sure the consistency of writing section titles. Consider the following example for the section titles.

3. Preliminaries
3.1. problem definition
3.2. State-of-the-art Solution
3.3. Indexing Framework: An augmented R-tree structure

Observe that those students cannot ensure the same style for writing those subtitles. "problem definition" are all in lower-case. The first letter of each word in "State-of-the-art Solution" are capitalized. The first letters of those words in "Indexing Framework: An augmented R-tree structure" can be either in lower-case or upper-case. Note that some students may think that these are just small mistakes. Why do we need to care much about them? Here, we need to emphasize that this mindset is incorrect. In the view point of reviewers, they can easily identify this issue because those titles (or subtitles) are normally bold and have the large font sizes. With these careless mistakes, reviewers can think that the authors may not be very careful for writing that paper. Worse still, reviewers can further determine that the authors may not be serious for writing that paper. Suppose that the authors do not care much about their paper. Why do reviewers need to care about it? As such, they can simply find reasons to reject it.

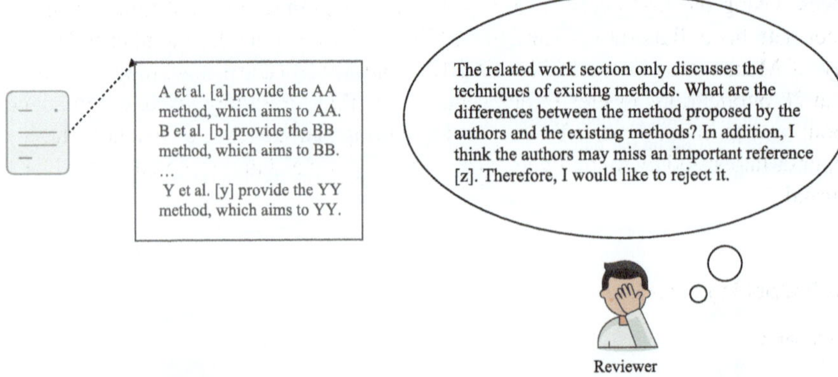

Fig. 5.17 A bad related work section simply lists all those related studies

5.9   Never Summarize and Identify Differences for Related Work

Many (junior) students simply list all those research studies in the related work section and do not identify the differences between these studies and their proposed solutions (see Fig. 5.17). Here, we need to point out that it is fine if those students are not familiar with the literature, i.e., they are still at the early stage (exploring stage) of handling a new research problem and have not proposed a new solution. However, if those students are in the middle stage/ending stage of handling this problem, i.e., they are familiar with those existing research studies and have ideas for a new solution, they should not write the related work section in this way. The main reason is that reviewers need to determine whether a research paper can advance the state of the art. If the related work section does not clearly show the differences between the proposed solution and existing methods, reviewers can think that it is not necessary to have yet another solution. Based solely on this reason, they can simply reject the paper.

Instead, the students should revise the related work section by (1) summarizing existing research papers into different groups and (2) pointing out the differences between the proposed solution and each of these groups (see Fig. 5.18). The main reason for categorizing these papers into different groups is that there are possibly many related papers in the field. For example, there are many research papers related to the function approximation approach. If students do not have these groups, reviewers can simply find any existing papers to attack their own research papers (e.g., paper [z] in Fig. 5.17). With these groups, even though reviewers can figure out one missing paper [z], they may not directly give rejection if the group that also covers [z] has been discussed in the related work section (see Fig. 5.18).

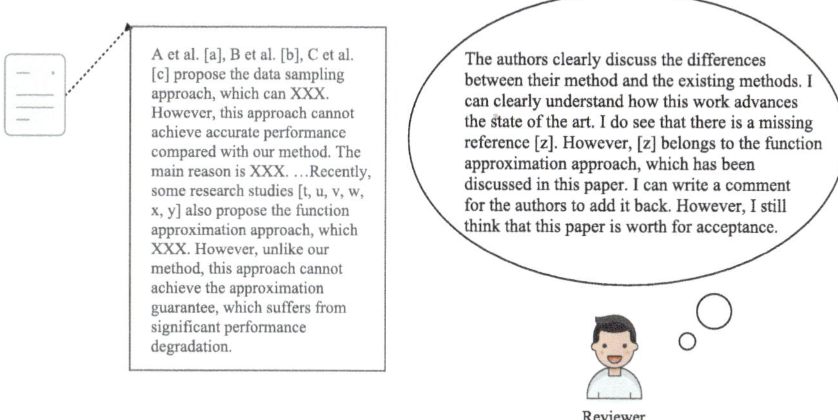

Fig. 5.18 A good related work needs to (1) categorize those existing papers into different groups and (2) point out the differences between the proposed solution and each of these groups

5.10 Too Much Background Information in the Introduction

Writing the Introduction section is often challenging for students. A common mistake is a lack of focus: some students spend more than two paragraphs discussing general background information without clearly stating the research problem or motivations. This can leave reviewers confused, as they are forced to read several unfocused paragraphs without understanding the purpose of the work. If reviewers have to work hard to figure out what the manuscript is about, it is likely to be rejected. We have encountered several manuscripts exhibiting this issue. Due to privacy concerns, we present an artificial example below.

Artificial intelligence (AI) has rapidly evolved over the last decade, becoming a major force in shaping industries and scientific discovery. As one of the key components of AI, machine learning has found success in areas such as finance, healthcare, robotics, and education. From personalized recommendations to autonomous vehicles, machine learning is making its presence felt in our daily lives.

Among various machine learning techniques, neural networks have played a pivotal role in driving progress. Their ability to learn hierarchical features from data has made them particularly suitable for tasks involving images, text, and audio. Over the years, researchers have explored different neural network architectures, from shallow models to deep networks with hundreds of layers.

Training algorithms, optimization techniques, and regularization methods have also seen significant improvements.

Backpropagation, gradient descent, batch normalization, and attention mechanisms are just a few of the key innovations that have contributed to the success of neural networks. With growing computational power and data availability, these models continue to evolve. In addition, transfer learning and pre-trained models such as BERT and GPT have further expanded the capabilities of neural networks in natural language processing.

In this paper, we explore ...

In the poorly written example above, the first three paragraphs talk broadly about AI, ML, and neural networks without narrowing down to a specific topic. Nowhere does it state what problem is being addressed, why it matters, or what previous methods fail to achieve. Why is this research important? Why now? Reviewers will not find any compelling reason to keep reading. Below, we show a rewritten, focused, and well-structured version of the poor example above.

Text classification is a fundamental task in natural language processing (NLP) with applications in sentiment analysis, topic detection, and spam filtering. Recent advances in neural network models, particularly large pre-trained language models such as BERT and GPT, have significantly improved performance on standard benchmarks. However, these models typically require large amounts of labeled data and extensive computational resources for fine-tuning, which limits their applicability in real-world scenarios where data is scarce.

In particular, few-shot text classification–where only a handful of labeled examples are available for each class–remains a challenging problem. While meta-learning and prompt-based methods have shown promise, they often rely on task-specific tuning or suffer from unstable performance across different domains. Moreover, existing models are often over-parameterized for low-data regimes, resulting in inefficiency and poor generalization.

To address these limitations, we propose ...

In this rewritten version, the introduction begins by presenting the broader task of text classification and recent advances. It then narrows the focus to few-shot text classification, explaining why this problem is important and challenging, and highlights the inefficiencies and instabilities of existing methods.

5.11 Solutions Do Not Address the Stated Challenges

When approaching a research problem, there are often multiple facets and challenges to consider. Some students attempt to highlight several of these issues in the Introduction section, aiming to demonstrate a comprehensive understanding of the problem space. However, a common mistake arises when the proposed methods or solutions presented later in the manuscript fail to address all the challenges previously outlined. This disconnect can confuse reviewers, who may expect the proposed work to provide solutions to all the identified problems. As a result, the manuscript may appear unfocused or incomplete, increasing the likelihood of rejection. We have observed this issue in several submitted manuscripts. To protect the confidentiality of the authors, we illustrate it with a constructed example below.

> Modern recommendation systems face a variety of challenges that limit their performance and applicability in real-world scenarios. These include: (1) Data sparsity, where users interact with only a small fraction of available items; (2) Cold-start problems, especially for new users or new items with no historical data; (3) Dynamic user preferences, which evolve over time and require models to adapt accordingly; and (4) Bias and fairness concerns, where recommendations may amplify popularity bias or marginalize minority users or items. Addressing all these challenges is critical for building robust and trustworthy recommendation systems.

This introduction sets a comprehensive stage, implying that the proposed method tackles a broad set of fundamental and well-known issues in recommendation. However, in the Methodology section, the authors present a graph-based collaborative filtering model that enhances user-item interaction modeling by learning representations over a user-item bipartite graph using graph neural networks (GNNs). The model achieves improved accuracy on standard recommendation benchmarks, but it does not include any mechanisms for: cold-start handling, temporal modeling of user preference dynamics, or bias mitigation.

This creates a clear misalignment between the problem framing and the actual contribution. Reviewers may raise concerns such as: "The introduction outlines several important challenges, but the method only addresses user-item interaction modeling," or "No empirical evidence is provided to support claims related to fairness, cold-start, or user preference drift." Such confusion can lead reviewers to question the focus of this paper and interpret the Introduction as overstating the contribution.

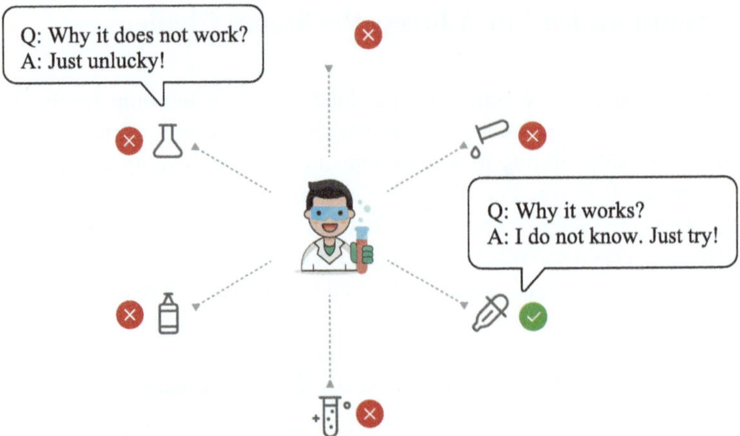

Fig. 5.19 Should have clear motivations for proposed methods

5.12 Unclear Motivation for Proposed Methods

When developing and designing methods for a research problem, some students tend to experiment with a few plausible approaches without carefully examining the underlying motivations. As shown in Fig. 5.19, if several methods fail, they may simply consider themselves unlucky. Conversely, if one approach happens to yield good results—often due to favorable data characteristics or tuning—they may quickly settle on that solution and begin writing a manuscript. In many cases, the resulting paper ends up as a straightforward description of the model architecture, followed by implementation steps and experimental outcomes, with little explanation of why the method was designed the way it was.

However, what makes a research paper compelling is not merely the final model, but the thought process that led to it. Readers and reviewers are often most interested in the intellectual journey: Why did you design the method this way? What challenge were you trying to address? What alternatives did you consider and why were they rejected? What core insight guided your decisions? These questions speak to the rationale and motivation behind the method, which are crucial for both scientific clarity and reader engagement.

A manuscript that lacks a clear discussion of the motivation and rationale behind the proposed method often feels shallow or unconvincing. Worse still, without a solid understanding of why the method works, it is difficult to judge whether it will generalize to datasets beyond those used in the paper. This undermines both the scientific value of the work and the confidence of the readers or reviewers in its broader applicability.

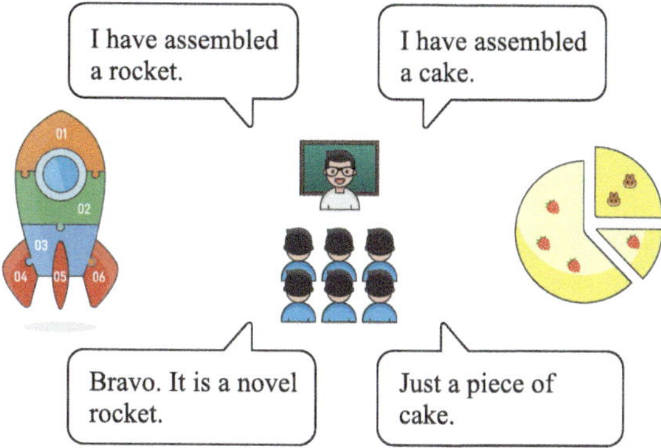

Fig. 5.20 Assemble a rocket versus assemble a cake

5.13   Propose a "New" Method by Naïvely Assembling Existing Techniques

Given a research problem, it is common for students to consider building a solution by assembling existing techniques. This strategy can be a valid way to propose a new method, particularly in areas where the reconfiguration or integration of established components can lead to improved performance, efficiency, or applicability. Indeed, many impactful works in machine learning and related fields are the result of carefully orchestrated combinations of prior methods. However, while assembling existing techniques can lead to novel insights, it also carries certain risks—especially when the assembly lacks innovation or depth.

As illustrated in Fig. 5.20, imagine two contrasting outcomes of the assembly approach. In the first case, the final method resembles a cake—an arrangement of well-known components that does not go beyond what is already well understood in the literature. The method may rely heavily on established modules, apply them in conventional ways, and introduce minimal or no new conceptual contributions. In such cases, reviewers may perceive the work as "a piece of cake"—that is, overly simplistic, obvious, or superficial. The lack of technical novelty or theoretical insight will likely lead to rejection, as the contribution does not meaningfully advance the field.

In the second case, the assembly results in something much more ambitious and integrated—like a rocket. Here, although the individual components may still be based on prior work, their combination is non-trivial. The integration requires careful engineering, deep understanding of each part, and possibly the development of new mechanisms to make them work together effectively. This type of work demonstrates creativity, technical depth, and a clear understanding of the problem space. Reviewers are more likely to recognize the novelty in how the components are combined, the challenges addressed during integration, and the new capabilities that emerge from the system as a whole. Such work is typically viewed as a meaningful contribution to the field.

Therefore, when proposing a new method by assembling existing techniques, it is essential to go beyond simply stacking modules together. One must articulate what is new in the combination, why the integration is necessary and non-trivial, and how it leads to a solution that could not have been achieved by naïvely applying the individual components in isolation. In essence, the difference between a cake and a rocket lies in the depth of thought, the degree of innovation, and the clarity of contribution that the assembly delivers.

Chapter 6
How to Enhance Your Chance for Making a Paper Accepted in a Top-Tier Venue?

In this chapter, we further discuss the correct mindsets for students in order to further enhance the chance for making a paper accepted in a top-tier venue, which can be summarized into the following six types.

6.1 Understand the Correct Positions of Reviewers and Authors

There are three main points that should be mentioned for the review process.

1. Reviewers are normally the professors and researchers, who have their own duties in their universities/research companies/research labs. They can be extremely busy.
2. Reviewers are volunteers, who are not paid by any organization.
3. Reviewers normally need to review a lot of papers at the same time. Using ICDE 2024 (second round) as an example, each reviewer needs to review roughly 18 papers (with 12 pages and IEEE double column format) in one and a half month.

Based on the above discussion, we expect that reviewers cannot spend a lot of time for reading each paper and have a right to reject a paper that they are not confident about the quality in a short period of time. Therefore, students should have the mindset that reviewers are the customers (or Kings and Queens) and they should be the ones who serve them. In other words, students should know the correct positions of reviewers and authors (see Fig. 6.1) so that they can change their attitudes for writing research papers.

© The Author(s) 2026
T. N. Chan and D. Wu, *Mastering the Academic Writing Mindset*,
https://doi.org/10.1007/978-981-95-4850-7_6

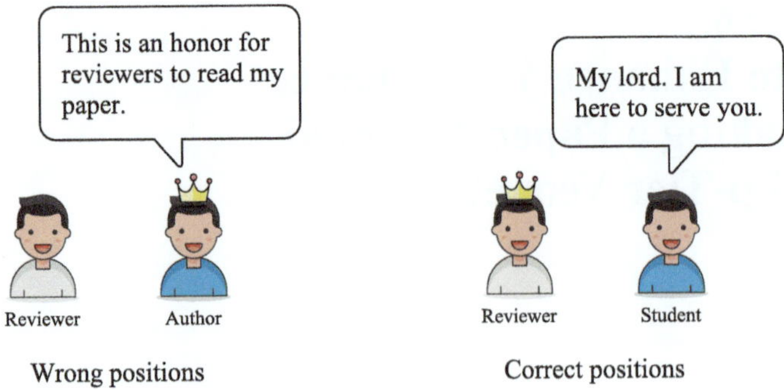

Fig. 6.1 Wrong and correct positions for reviewers and authors

6.2 Understand the Conferences/Journals

Every conference/journal has its own scope and target readers, which are normally listed in its webpage. Students should check carefully about this information in the webpage before they choose to submit a paper in that conference/journal. Using ICDE 2025 as an example (see Fig. 6.2),[1] this conference explicitly mentions that it does not accept a paper that purely advances the machine learning model without any data management issues. Therefore, students should not submit anything about this to this conference. Otherwise, the acceptance chance is zero and there will be no meaningful comments from reviewers (i.e., this is a waste of time.). In addition, students should also check those papers from the target conferences/journals and understand the research/writing styles from them. The main reason is that reviewers

Desk Rejection Policy

ICDE research track submissions that don't meet the following requirements may be rejected without review.

Submissions must follow the aforementioned **guidelines** and **length** requirements specified in the ICDE 2025 Call for Papers.

Submissions **must be in scope** of ICDE 2025. Specifically, this means that **a submission must align with at least one of the above topic areas** defined for ICDE 2025 and **situate itself within the state of the art of current and past research in the database community in general and within the selected topic(s) in particular.** For example, submissions that purely advance machine learning approaches not relating to any data management aspects (e.g. scalability and efficiency) would be considered as not in scope of ICDE.

Fig. 6.2 Each conference/journal has its own policy/scope for accepting papers. Do not submit papers to the venues that do not match together. This figure is obtained from the official webpage of ICDE 2025

---

[1] The link is https://ieee-icde.org/2025/cfp/.

will normally reject those papers that do not match their styles. For example, if those venues love those papers related to AI/ML, it is hard for them to accept some papers related to system development. Using the first author of this book as an example, he submitted one paper about using the piecewise-linear function to improve the efficiency for training SVM models with additive kernels to the data management venues (SIGMOD, VLDB, and ICDE). Although this paper is still within the scope of these venues, those reviewers were not very keen to this paper and mentioned that this topic is not interesting. Once he submitted this paper to TKDE, in which the research style aligns with that paper, he first got a revision and then got an acceptance.

6.3 Understand Five Main Reject Reasons by Reviewers

In order to reject a paper by a top-tier conference/journal, reviewers normally need to provide at least one of these five main reasons, which are (1) lack of motivation, (2) limited novelty/technical contribution, (3) weak presentation, (4) insufficient related work, and (5) missing a lot of important experiments. Therefore, once the students think that they are confident for avoiding all these reasons, their papers can have a relatively high chance to be accepted in a top-tier conference/journal. Here, we discuss how to avoid these reject reasons.

Lack of motivation. When the student writes everything, they need to provide a clear motivation. Then, some students may raise this question. How to provide motivation? Our answer is "always ask questions". Suppose that the student wants to work on one research topic. They need to immediately raise the following questions.

- What are the applications for this topic?
- Who are the users?
- How do the users use this?
- What are the challenges for this problem/topic?
- (For old topic) There have been some existing research studies. Why do you need to make another solution? (Is it more accurate? Is it more efficient?)
- (For new topic) No one has studied this before. Why do you need to be the first to study this topic? (Solid motivation should be provided.)

If the students can clearly answer all the above questions, they can tell a complete story of their work. We can state that their research topics are clearly motivated. If the students cannot provide concrete answers, they need to think deeply about the answers in order to motivate their research topics.

Limited novelty/technical contribution. This comment is somehow the most difficult one for students (even for some faculty members). In order to avoid this comment, students need to read various papers in the target venues in order to understand the technical depth. Here, we provide two strategies for avoiding this comment.

<u>Find new problems/settings</u>. We would like to emphasize that reviewers are normally lenient to those research papers that focus on new research problems (or new settings). The reason is that the paper looks new starting from the early stage (problem/setting). Therefore, we encourage that students should think of a new problem rather than conducting research in an old problem (e.g., similarity search based on Euclidean distance, which has been done three decades ago). In other words, students should not simply follow others. With a new problem/setting, it is also easy for students to think of novel solutions with solid technical contributions due to the lack of competitors.

<u>Find interdisciplinary research problems that are not sufficiently considerable by researchers in the computer science field</u>. Using the first author of this book as an example, he worked on the research problem of developing efficient algorithms for Kernel Density Visualization (KDV). Although KDV is mainly used in GIS/geography communities, it is also related to spatiotemporal data management in the computer science field. However, there is a lack of researchers in computer science who focus on this problem. As such, there is a big room for him to develop efficient solutions for handling this problem and its variants. In addition, other researchers also do not care about this problem at that time. With these reasons, he can publish many top-tier papers in the data management/data mining venues that are related to this problem.

Weak presentation. When students write papers, they need to have this word in mind, which is "connection". If a paper is disconnected, it is very hard for readers to understand the flow of the paper. Here, we provide some examples of common mistakes.

Example 1 Some students have provided the problem definition in Section 2 and have mentioned one method in Section 3. However, the proposed method does not have enough linkage with the problem definition. Therefore, this can let readers raise the question for whether this method is really solving the problem.

Example 2 Some students first present the method A and then the method B. However, there is no linkage between these two methods. Therefore, readers can raise the concern for why they need to propose two methods but not the best one.

Example 3 Some students discuss existing methods in the "Preliminaries" section and present their new method without any reason (i.e., loses the linkage between the existing methods and the new method). Therefore, readers may wonder why they need to develop this new method.

In order to avoid the above mistakes, we emphasize that students need to make sure that everything is connected naturally when they are writing research papers. Once the students achieve this goal, they can easily address this comment.

Insufficient related work. Students need to make sure that they can provide a comprehensive survey for their research topics. Using the first author of this book as an example, he classifies the related work into different categories. For each category,

Fig. 6.3 The first author of this book plans for the experiments in advance so that he does not miss some important experiments before the paper submission

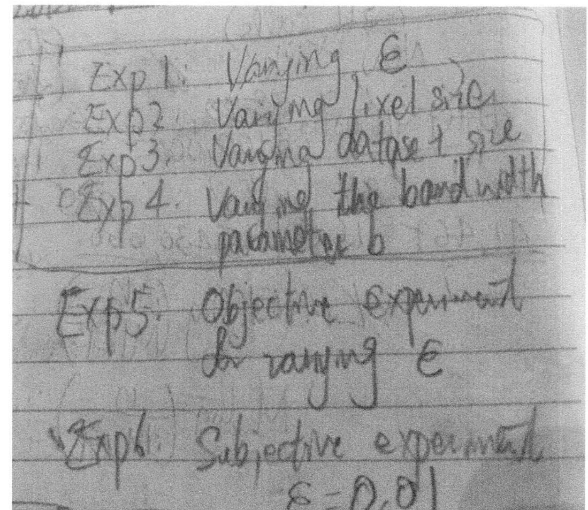

he provides excessive references in prestigious conferences/journals (most of them are published recently) and mentions the differences between each category and his method. There are two main advantages for this approach. First, it is very hard for reviewers to figure out some missing references. Second, even though reviewers have identified a missing reference, it can belong to one of the categories, which indicates that this reference still has the same differences compared with his method. As such, it is hard for reviewers to use this reason to reject the paper.

Missing a lot of important experiments. Many (junior) students may not think carefully about which experiments they need to conduct when they prepare for their research papers. As such, they may have missed a lot of important experiments when they reach the deadline of submission. Here, we suggest that they provide the plan for which experiments they need to conduct in the first place. Consider the first author of this book as an example. When he worked on a research topic, he had the plan for conducting which experiments in advance (see Fig. 6.3). Observe that he clearly wrote down which variable he should vary in each experiment. Once this plan is ready, what he needs to do is to write down the script file to vary this variable for testing the performance.

6.4 Deal with Revision

If a student is lucky to have a chance for revision, we need to congratulate him/her because it is highly possible that the paper can be accepted in the conference or journal. In the rule of thumb, the acceptance rate is normally more than 80% if a revision is granted for a paper. As an example, the acceptance rate of VLDB 2015

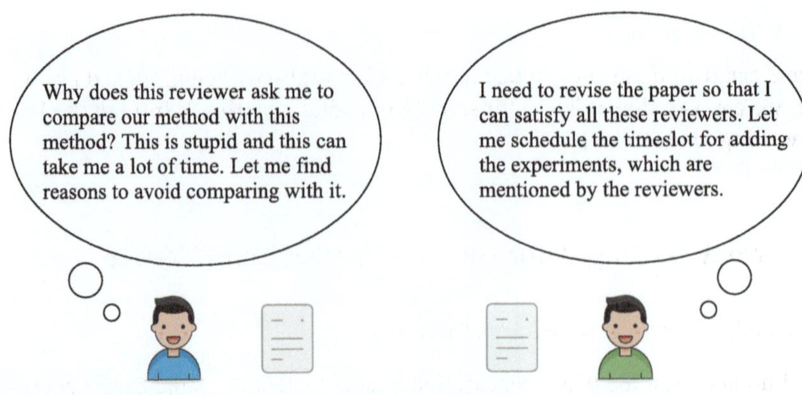

Fig. 6.4 The correct and wrong approaches for handling the comments from reviewers in a revision

is 84.6% after revision. Therefore, students need to be very serious about the revision. Figure 6.4 shows the correct and wrong approaches for students to deal with the revision.

In a revision, the reviewer can possibly ask some questions for the authors to change the paper (e.g., add additional experiments or change the presentation). Some students may be very annoyed about these comments because they need to spend more time to deal with them (by implementing some methods or thinking of new structures for writing the papers). Therefore, they will tend to pass over these questions by finding some excuses to avoid doing it. Here, we need to emphasize that this mindset is completely wrong. If the reviewer has already provided concrete (and doable) experiments (e.g., ask the students to add the running-time experiment by changing the dataset size), the students need to add it either in the response letter, in the paper, or in the technical report no matter whether this experiment is meaningful or not. They need to know that reviewers are the ones who can determine the acceptance/rejection of a paper. They are Kings and Queens. Therefore, in order to make a paper accepted, all they need to do is to make them happy (satisfied). If they figure out that the authors (i.e., the students) do not have the intension to address their comments, they can feel very angry and give a rejection.

Figure 6.5 provides an analogy for dealing with revision. A student needs to act as a servant who serves for a customer (i.e., a reviewer). As a servant, all he/she needs to do is to make the customer happy. Once the customer is happy, the servant can receive some benefits from the customer (e.g., tips). Otherwise, the customer can be angry and writes a complaint letter so that the servant can lose the job.

Fig. 6.5 This is an analogy for dealing with a revision. A productive student (upper one) needs to act as a servant to make a reviewer (i.e., a customer (or a king)) happy, while an unproductive student (lower one) makes a reviewer (i.e., a customer (or a king)) angry

6.5   The More Papers You Submit, the More "Accept" You Get

Many students may wonder how to submit a paper so that they can ensure that the paper must be accepted in the conference/journal. Here, we would like to point out that we can only try our best to improve the research paper. However, we cannot say that there is a 100% chance for a paper to be accepted in a top-tier venue after we submit that paper (even though we have followed all those suggestions in this book). There are two main reasons.

The acceptance rate of top-tier venues is normally low. Many top-tier venues, including SIGMOD, SIGKDD, VLDB, and ICDE, have the acceptance rate of 15–30%. As an example, the acceptance rate of SIGKDD 2025 (February Cycle) is only 18.4% (see Fig. 6.6). Therefore, we need to expect that we can only have one paper accepted in this conference once we have submitted five papers on average.

The authors in top-tier venues are mostly from top universities/research labs. Note that top-tier venues are very competitive. Many researchers in top universities/research labs (e.g., MIT, Stanford, Harvard, Tsinghua, and AT&T lab) also submit papers to these venues. Since these researchers can possibly be the best of the best in the world, this can further increase the difficulties for a paper (of a newbie with a lack of experience) to be accepted in these venues.

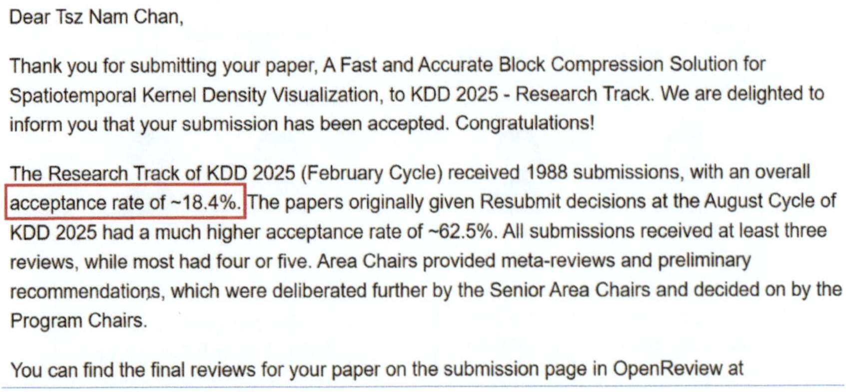

Dear Tsz Nam Chan,

Thank you for submitting your paper, A Fast and Accurate Block Compression Solution for Spatiotemporal Kernel Density Visualization, to KDD 2025 - Research Track. We are delighted to inform you that your submission has been accepted. Congratulations!

The Research Track of KDD 2025 (February Cycle) received 1988 submissions, with an overall acceptance rate of ~18.4%. The papers originally given Resubmit decisions at the August Cycle of KDD 2025 had a much higher acceptance rate of ~62.5%. All submissions received at least three reviews, while most had four or five. Area Chairs provided meta-reviews and preliminary recommendations, which were deliberated further by the Senior Area Chairs and decided on by the Program Chairs.

You can find the final reviews for your paper on the submission page in OpenReview at

Fig. 6.6   The acceptance rate of SIGKDD 2025 (February Cycle) is only 18.4%

Based on the above reasons, some students may observe that their hard work for submitting many papers seems to be useless and may raise this question. Does it mean that they should not work hard for submitting many papers? The answer is no. Here, we would like to use the probability concept to explain this. Suppose that the probability of acceptance for each submission is p. If the student has n papers for submission. Obviously, the expected value of acceptance is $n \times p$, based on the concept of Binomial distribution. Therefore, if the number of submissions n is larger, the number of acceptances must also be larger (given that p is not zero). Here, we consider the first author of this book as an example (see Fig. 6.7). In 2024, he had submitted seven papers to the VLDB conference (with the acceptance rate of roughly 20%). Note that only two papers are accepted in this conference. As such, the number of accepted papers is just slightly higher than the expected number ($7 \times 0.2 = 1.4$). Hence, each student needs to know that "the more papers you submit, the more "accept" you get". This statement is true regardless of which venues the student targets for. Furthermore, the value p (i.e., the probability of acceptance) can increase once students submit more papers to top-tier venues (by obtaining meaningful comments and gaining more experience). Therefore, every student should aim to submit papers to top-tier venues.

6.6   Never Give Up

Many students can get a lot of rejections for each of their research papers until they make that paper accepted in the conference/journal. Normally, there are three kinds of attitudes for those students once they receive a rejection notification (see Fig. 6.8). First, some students may think that this is the end of the world and have a doubt for whether they are suitable to be a qualified researcher. They will give up very easily (i.e., have no passion for doing anything related to research). Ultimately,

Fig. 6.7 This is how the first author of this book submitted papers to VLDB 2024. Note that the more he submits, the more "Accept" he gets

Ending: This student graduates with no paper and leaves the academia forever.

Ending: This student graduates with many second-tier/third-tier publications. No university wants to recruit this student.

Ending: This student graduates with four top-tier publications and still has six unpublished papers that are under submission (to top-tier venues).

Fig. 6.8 A productive student keeps submitting papers to top-tier venues no matter how many "Reject" they receive

they will leave the academia after graduation (some of them may even give up their postgraduate degrees). Second, some ("better") students may be willing to submit that paper. But they choose some second-tier or third-tier venues (a.k.a. easy venues). Ultimately, no university wants to hire them after graduation because of the concern for whether they can conduct good research. Third, the best students insist for submitting papers to top-tier venues (no matter how many rejections they receive). Only these students can get a lot of top-tier papers after graduation and can be recruited by a top university/research lab.

To the first two types of research students, we would like to emphasize that the acceptance rate of top-tier venues is only 15–30% (as discussed in Sect. 6.5). Since the probability of acceptance is lower than 0.5, you need to expect that each research paper can be rejected for each submission. Despite this, each paper can ultimately be accepted once you keep submitting it based on the following probability concept.

Suppose that the probability of acceptance for each submission is p (where $p > 0$). The probability of acceptance in the ith submission is $(1 - p)^{i-1} p$ (i.e., get rejections for $i - 1$ times and get acceptance for the ith time). Therefore, the probability of acceptance for a paper when the student keeps submitting it to top-tier venues is expressed as follows.

$$\sum_{i=1}^{\infty} (1 - p)^{i-1} p = p + (1 - p)p + (1 - p)^2 p + \cdots$$

$$= p(1 + (1 - p) + (1 - p)^2 + \cdots) = p\left(\frac{1}{1 - (1 - p)}\right) = 1$$

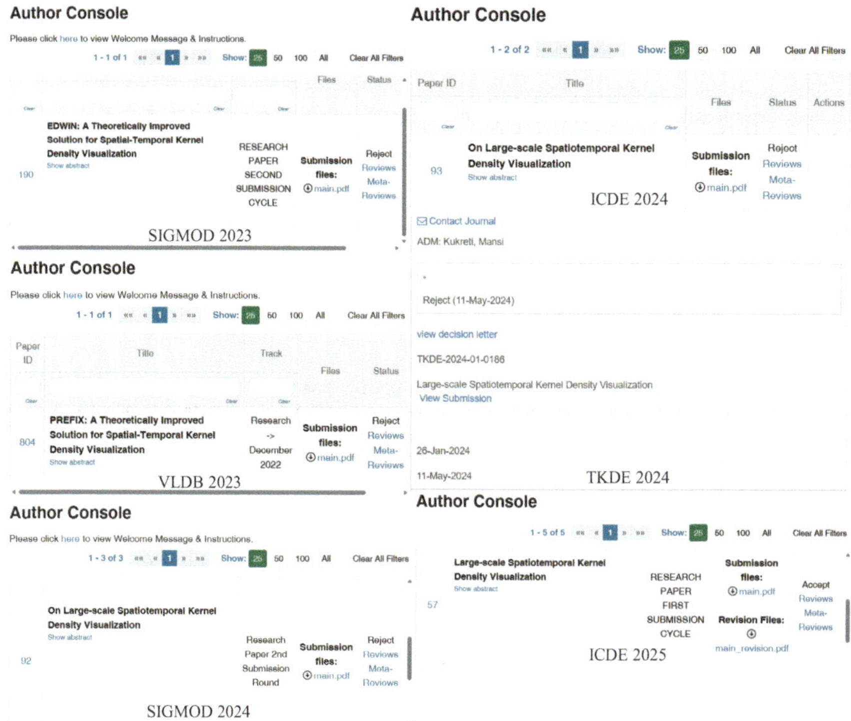

Fig. 6.9 The first author of this book gets five times of rejection and ultimately manages to get the acceptance from ICDE 2025 for one of his research papers

With this expression, if the student keeps submitting one paper, that paper must be ultimately accepted as long as the probability of acceptance for each submission p is not zero. This expression holds regardless of which venue the student targets for. As an example, although p can be smaller for a top-tier venue, the probability of acceptance is still 1 if the student keeps submitting that paper. Based on this reason, each student should choose top-tier venues for submission. Figure 6.9 illustrates an example for how the first author of this book submits the paper (regarding the efficient algorithms for spatiotemporal kernel density visualization) to top-tier venues. He finished this work in July 2022 and submitted this paper to SIGMOD 2023. The reviewers were negative about this work and gave a reject for it. He kept revising this paper (the title was changed) and submitted it to VLDB 2023 in December 2022 but it was still rejected. He did not give up and submitted it to SIGMOD 2024 and then ICDE 2024 (the title was changed again.) and was rejected again and again. He further revised the paper (the title was changed again.) and submitted it to TKDE 2024 and was still rejected. Lastly, he submitted it to ICDE 2025. This time, he got an acceptance in November 2024 for this paper. We believe that many students (or even faculty members) may have already given up this paper if they have received many rejections for one paper. This example shows that we should never give up. The paper must be accepted in top-tier venues if we keep revising and submitting it.